NORWICH CITY COLLEGE LIBRARY

Stock No.	171433
Class	64E
Cat.	Pro

KT-471-506

A chef's guide to nutrition

Hilary Balmforth

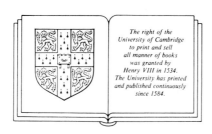

The right of the
University of Cambridge
to print and sell
all manner of books
was granted by
Henry VIII in 1534.
The University has printed
and published continuously
since 1584.

CAMBRIDGE UNIVERSITY PRESS

Cambridge

New York   Port Chester   Melbourne   Sydney

171   433

Published by the Press Syndicate of the University of Cambridge
The Pitt Building, Trumpington Street, Cambridge CB2 1RP
40 West 20th Street, New York, NY 10011-4211, USA
10 Stamford Road, Oakleigh, Victoria 3166, Australia

© Cambridge University Press 1992

First published 1992

Printed in Great Britain by Scotprint Ltd, Musselburgh, Scotland

British Library cataloguing in publication data
Balmforth, Hilary
A chef's guide to nutrition.
1. Nutrition
I. Title
613.2

ISBN 0 521 38886 4

Text illustrations by Gordon Hendry

Notice to teachers
The contents of this book are in the copyright of Cambridge University
Press.
Unauthorised copying of any of the pages is not only illegal but also goes
against the interests of the author.
For authorised copying please check that your school has a licence
(through the local education authority) from the Copyright Licensing
Agency which enables you to copy small parts of the text in limited
numbers.

Acknowledgements
The author and publisher would like to thank the following for their kind
permission to reproduce material in this book: p. 74 Heinemann Publishers
(Oxford) Ltd; p. 76 HMSO.

Contents

Preface

Having spent many years working with food, it has never ceased to amaze me how far down their list of priorities those working in the catering industry place nutrition. Nutrition does not figure in the planning of menus, nor in the preparing, cooking and serving of food to the general public. When, six years ago, I became involved in the training of chefs and caterers, I realized that perhaps one reason for this was the way we taught it in college and the lack of information available for the would-be chef.

Nutrition is a complex science, still young as sciences go, and still in a state of change as advanced technology grapples with complex processes as to what food contains and how the human body utilizes it. We know a lot, but there are still vast areas to explore. This is for the experts to tackle; our job as caterers is to translate these findings into food on the plate for our customers.

During the past decade it has become clear that there is a definite relationship between the food we eat and our health. The catering industry can play a major part in influencing the choices customers make in their diet and can thereby help prevent food-related diseases.

This book is an attempt to right the wrong by providing basic information on nutrition which a chef will require in his/her work. The aim is to apply the science of nutrition to the food on the plate and show ways in which modern thinking about health can be interpreted in practical ways that the chef can follow and develop.

No book can be written in isolation and this one was no exception. To my long-suffering colleagues in the Catering Sector of Cambridge Regional College I say a very big 'thank you'. Without their help, interest and encouragement the book would not have been written. Many of them acted as 'sounding boards' for ideas and helped in the research. I am very grateful for their thoughtfulness and concern and I can only hope they approve of the result! To family and close friends also go many thanks for showing such interest, consideration and support, all of which was greatly appreciated.

A final word to the reader. I hope that on completing the book you will have a much clearer idea of what nutrition is all about and how it can be applied to your everyday work of providing food for the customers you cater for. If this is so the aim has been achieved.

one **What makes us eat?**

Human beings do have some similarities. We may not look alike, we may have different hobbies and interests in life, we may be short, tall, big-boned or petite but one thing we do have in common is that we all eat food. How much food we eat can vary between individuals, as can how often and when we eat. Sadly, the amount and variety of food available is different in different parts of the world: food choices are generally far more limited in the poorer countries. In Britain we are fortunate in having a wide range of easily available foods to tempt our palate. But what drives us to eat? What makes us choose particular foods?

Factors affecting our choice of food

Hunger

This is one of the driving forces behind man's survival. The 'drive mechanism' for hunger is situated at the base of the brain and is triggered off by a series of chemical stimuli. It is a complex system not fully understood but it is known that humans can survive for a number of weeks without eating food although the body must have a daily supply of fluids. But is hunger the main reason why we eat or choose certain foods? In drought-ridden areas of the world, where food is scarce, hunger and the need for survival are major factors. In Britain we are spoilt for choice: there is a plentiful supply of foods ranging from basic commodities to exotic fare, so the drive for survival and the need to eat to live is diminished.

The human body is a very complex machine but strangely there appears to be no system whereby the body can determine which foods it requires to give it the necessary nourishment. For example, if the body wishes to build more muscle tissue, the brain cannot send out signals to make us eat the foods which will provide us with the necessary ingredients for making tissue. Similarly there is no mechanism to tell us to stop eating sugary foods to prevent tooth decay. Instead we carry on eating such foods and only stop when it is probably too late and we are suffering from toothache!

So although there is a drive mechanism for hunger it would appear to be limited in the influence it has on our choice of food. It can, however, determine the quantity of food we eat by deactivating or 'switching off' when food is in the stomach and small intestine and we experience that 'full' feeling and stop eating. Some people's capacity for food is greater than others' and it would appear that in these cases the brain may have its wires crossed as to when to call a halt. There are times when all of us suffer what we term 'hunger pangs' – when, for example, we are late for a meal or have missed out a meal completely. Can we really term these feelings hunger or are they the result of some other factor?

Habit

This probably accounts for some of those 'hunger pangs'. Much of our eating is based on habit. We tend to eat at certain times of the day and our body appears to adjust accordingly. Many people in Britain eat two to three times a day with drinks and snacks in between; other people eat once a day while yet others nibble continuously. Whichever way we choose, it becomes a habit. Any change in the pattern will bring about a response by the body until the 'new' habit is established.

What we choose to eat can also be habit-forming. We get used to a certain taste in food whether it be sweet or savoury and that can determine our choice to the point where we may not be willing to change or experiment with different flavours.

Family eating habits

Foods which have been familiar to us for most of our lives can influence our choice. The foods we were given as children can form the basis of our diet when we are older. The way we eat and the type of meals we consume within the family unit can have a marked effect on our choice of food. This response can be negative as well as positive. Continual repetition of certain foods can cause us to develop strong dislikes as we grow older.

Peer group eating

Our friends and those in the same age group as us also influence our choice of food. This is particularly significant with young children and teenagers, especially the former. For example, at a birthday party for a small boy, one young guest would not eat the sardine sandwiches. Consequently all the young guests decided they too would not eat sardine sandwiches, much to the embarrassment of the harassed mother! As we grow older, however, individual choices on food tend to dominate more.

Culture

There are certain dishes which appear to symbolize Britain, such as roast beef and Yorkshire pudding, and fish and chips, to give just two examples. Dishes like these are part of our culture as far as food is concerned. Other food traditions are linked to festive occasions such as Christmas and Easter, or weddings and parties: for example, Christmas pudding, Easter eggs, wedding cake.

Climate

In Britain, as in other parts of northern Europe, we live in a climate which

is ideally suited to rearing animals and growing crops. This influences the choice of foods in our diet, by determining what foods are available. For example, meat and dairy products, along with bread and cakes, form the basis of our diet whereas in southern Italy, which is too hot to rear many animals, the basic diet consists of vegetables, fruit and pasta.

Climate also influences us at a personal level. In cold weather, for example, we are inclined to eat hot foods and foods which are satisfying and filling, whereas in hot weather our appetite decreases and we enjoy cold foods.

Taste, colour and texture of food

These are very important in determining our likes and dislikes in food. Taste can be influenced by family eating habits and peer groups as discussed earlier. Children are more conservative about food whereas adults are more willing to experiment.

When a dish looks attractive we are more inclined to want to eat it, and a meal is more tempting if the individual dishes are recognizable and not just a mess on the plate. The palatability of food is all important, that is when it is 'pleasant to the taste' or 'agreeable to the mind'. The presentation of food – the colour, texture and appearance – is crucial in determining what we are prepared to eat, a point to which we shall return when considering menu planning in Chapter 10.

Moods

Our moods can influence our choice of food and also when we eat. Many people eat more food when they are feeling bored or upset, something which can be described as 'eating for comfort' as we use food as a means of consolation. We associate some foods with happy times in our lives. Such foods become favourites whereas others remind us of sad or unhappy experiences and become foods which we dislike.

Budget

This is obviously a determining factor: the more money we have available to buy food, the more our choice will be enhanced and the greater the variety we can enjoy. When eating out in a restaurant, many people will choose foods which are not readily available to them on a daily basis and which could be quite expensive. Their choice will include 'luxury' foods and they will also experiment with new and tantalizing flavours. Other people will keep to more familiar foods even when dining out on a special occasion and these foods could be relatively inexpensive.

Availability of food

This is important when we are considering choices of foods. The greater variety of foods available to us, the wider our choice can be.

We have looked at a number of factors which influence our food choices. When and which foods we eat is also affected by our eating habits as well as a number of social pressures.

How our eating habits are developed

We are not born with eating habits: they develop as a result of learned behaviour from the time we are born and are altered to suit our given circumstances throughout our lifetime. The learning process is unconscious; we are not actually aware of it.

What are eating habits? They are our daily eating patterns and include:

- the food we choose to eat
- how many, how large and what types of meals we eat
- with whom we eat these meals
- how those meals are prepared and cooked
- the time of day they are consumed.

All these factors are in their turn influenced by the traditions and culture of the community that the individual is a part of.

The family unit, and particularly the mother, is the strongest influence on a young child when it is initially acquiring patterns of eating. The child learns about when to eat and which foods are acceptable and a system of meals develops. Food also takes on emotional implications when it is used for comfort, rewards and presents: these will be important throughout our lives. A box of chocolates is a favourite present; many of us raid the kitchen cupboards when we are bored or upset; and one way of celebrating is to go out for a meal.

These initial family food patterns are further modified by other additional influences such as school, peer groups, other individuals and changing circumstances. For example, when the child is older the mother may return to work and the family eating patterns may change to accommodate the different circumstances. Or a change from primary school to secondary school with a different system of lunches will enforce a change in eating habits.

Modifications in eating habits occur throughout a person's lifetime and may be brought about by such transitions as going to college, starting work, changing jobs, getting married, having children, children leaving home, and old age. These modifications can take the form of changes in food choices, number of meals, types of meals and cooking methods.

Social influences on eating habits

Social pressures are some of the most interesting influences on our eating habits. This is of particular concern to the catering industry and to us as food handlers. We now have more leisure time in this country than ever before, and this is increasingly being filled by social activities. The interesting fact is that whatever the social activity, whether it is a sport, disco dancing or just an evening with friends, food and/or drink is involved. It is rare for a friend who comes to visit not to be offered some form of hospitality, even if this comprises just a cup of tea or coffee and a biscuit. When we go out to meet friends some part of that time will be spent consuming food and drink. In fact eating out has become a leisure activity in its own right with people spending time over a meal in a restaurant, trying out new gastronomic experiences. If we celebrate, food is also involved. All this illustrates how food plays a much more significant part in our lives than just keeping us alive.

The social influences on eating habits have proved very useful in promoting the expansion of the catering industry. The number of restaurants and fast-food outlets has increased in recent years along with leisure activities. A recent Gallup poll showed that in 1986, 43 per cent of the population of Britain ate out socially each month. This has important implications for jobs within the industry, and it also gives the caterer an additional role. This new role entails not just providing a service to the customer but also taking a more active interest in their nutritional well-being.

Religious, moral and medical influences on eating habits

Religion

Many of the world's religions cater not only for the individual's spiritual needs but also for their overall well-being, and this is reflected in specific dietary laws. Some religions are based on the sanctity of life and the passing, after death, of a soul from one body to another, known as transmigration. These factors too will affect an individual's food choices. Below are listed the major religions which have dietary laws.

Hinduism
Orthodox followers of this religion are vegetarians as two of the main concepts are the sanctity of life and transmigration. Therefore the eating of meat is not allowed and the diet consists of plant foods and animal products which do not involve killing. However, strict Hindus will not eat eggs as these are considered to be a potential source of life. Hindus consider that the cow is sacred and a pig is unclean. Less orthodox Hindus are not strict vegetarians and will eat meat and fish but never beef or pork.

Sikhism
The dietary laws in this religion are less strict than those of Hinduism and eggs and meat are permitted. However, the cow is still considered sacred and therefore beef is not eaten and pork is deemed to be unclean. Slaughtering of animals is permitted if this is done by a single blow to the head. The meat produced by this method is known as 'khatka' meat.

Islam

Followers of this religion are known as Muslims and it is said that over a third of the world's population are believers. The teachings of Islam are written in the Koran and cover all aspects of life including dietary laws. Muslims can eat meat but not pork as the pig is considered unclean. They eat poultry and fish but not shellfish as these are also considered unclean. The animals have to be ritually slaughtered and the meat is known as 'halal' meat.

Buddhism

This religion teaches the way of liberation through ethics and discipline, including meditation. All Buddhists are vegetarian and do not eat any animal flesh. Some are vegan and only eat plant food and no animal products at all.

Rastafarianism

This religion is practised by some West Indians, and their dietary laws prohibit the eating of any animal or animal product. Strict Rastafarians are vegans.

Judaism

The religion of the Jews is the oldest monotheistic religion and encompasses all aspects of an individual's life. The dietary laws arise out of the Mosaic law, given in the books of the Bible known as Deuteronomy and Leviticus. The main laws state that a Jew must not eat meat from an unclean animal and should only eat meat from animals with cloven hooves who chew the cud – so beef, lamb and venison can be eaten but not pork. Poultry and fish with scales and fins ('round' fish such as cod, haddock, herring, salmon and trout) can be eaten, but 'flat' fish, shellfish and other fish which eat on the sea-bed are forbidden. Also a Jew must not eat blood. The animal is slaughtered by having its jugular vein cut and the blood is then allowed to drain from the carcass. The meat is butchered in such a way as to remove all the veins and arteries: it is then known as kosher meat. Orthodox Jews will not have meat and dairy products at the same meal.

These are just some examples of the way the world's religions have their own diets. They will all affect the choices of foods which the individual follower can make.

Moral issues

A number of people in this country are turning away from eating meat and fish and becoming vegetarians or vegans. The former may eat some animal products such as milk, butter, cheese and yogurt while vegans only eat plant food. Moral considerations often lie behind this change. Many people are against modern agricultural methods, especially the ways animals are slaughtered for food, as well as the intensive farming of poultry, cattle, pigs and fish, which is considered to be cruel.

Medical factors

More people are becoming conscious of their health and are aware that the food they eat can affect their fitness. Many have turned to a vegetarian or vegan diet while others have cut down their intake of fatty foods. However, there are many people who are forced to make adjustments to the types of food they eat for medical reasons. If they are overweight, their doctor may advise them to lose weight, which will mean they must change their eating habits. A diabetic must alter his or her diet as part of the medical treatment of the condition. High blood pressure and high cholesterol levels in the blood are conditions which will involve a change in food choices to help alleviate the problem. There are a number of other medical conditions that can develop during our lifetime which will require an alteration in our choice of food.

This chapter has tried to highlight the reasons why we choose certain foods and has examined some of the factors behind our choices. Eating, which on the surface seems such a straightforward process, is in fact highly complex and involves many outside influences on choices of food and eating habits. This area of nutrition, known as **social nutrition**, is very important to a chef who has to cater for customers with many varied tastes in food. It is also important to keep in mind these fundamental ideas on eating habits and food choices when studying the basics of nutrition and developing criteria for menu planning and sensible eating.

Checksheet

Try to answer the following questions.

1. List the ten major factors which influence our choice of foods:
   a.
   b.
   c.
   d.
   e.
   f.
   g.
   h.
   i.
   j.

2. Eating habits are determined in childhood. True or false.

3. In 1986, the percentage of the population of Britain eating out socially was:
   a. 33 per cent   *b.* 43 per cent   *c.* 53 per cent   *d.* 63 per cent

4. An orthodox Hindu will eat meat.   True or false.

5. A Sikh will not eat beef.   True or false.

6. A Muslim will not eat pork.   True or false.

7. A Buddhist is a vegetarian.   True or false.

8. Rastafarians are meat eaters.   True or false.

9. State the three main dietary laws of Judaism:
   a.
   b.
   c.

10. The name given to the meat after the ritual slaughter of animals in Islam is _____.

Now turn to the text to check your answers.

Further study

Complete the following tasks.

1. List the dishes which you consider to be typical of Britain. It may help to subdivide your list into dishes for England, Wales, Scotland and Northern Ireland. Why do you think there are differences in dishes between the areas?

2. Now carry out the same exercise for some other countries. Give your reasons for the choice of dishes you make for each country.

3. Produce a questionnaire to determine the social trends that underlie the eating patterns of your fellow students. Include questions on the types of meals taken, number of meals per day, food choices, number of meals per week taken outside the home, snack meals, etc. Present your results in the form of a chart or graph.

4. Choose one of the religions discussed in Chapter 1 and research the history of that religion in depth indicating the reasons behind its dietary laws. List the foods which can be eaten and those which need to be avoided by a strict believer.

5. Discover if there is a member of your college group who is a vegetarian. Interview that person to discover the reasons for this, and list the foods which can and cannot be eaten by vegetarians.

6. Imagine you are invited out to a restaurant for dinner and the chef has agreed to cook you a three-course meal of your choice with no expense spared. Write down the meal you would ask the chef to prepare for you. Look carefully at your choices and list the reasons you consider influenced you to choose those dishes and not others. Compare your reasons with those discussed.

two Examining nutrition

Before we look in detail at food and what it consists of, it is worth while spending a short time defining certain terms that crop up in the study of nutrition.

We should perhaps start by trying to define the term **nutrition**. Nutrition is basically the 'study of food in relation to the needs of living organisms' (Arnold E. Bender, *Dictionary of Nutrition and Food Technology*, 1968). It is a many-faceted discipline, incorporating other sciences such as physiology, biochemistry, chemistry, and physics as well as medicine, agriculture and food science. Nutrition can be applied to all living organisms but in catering we are primarily concerned with human nutrition – an area of nutrition which, as William Scheider puts it in his *Nutrition, Basic Concepts and Applications*, 'studies the means by which we obtain, assimilate and utilize food'. **Human nutrition** covers the nature of food; what food consists of; which foods are important to us; how much food we need; factors influencing the availability of food and our choice of foods; the effect of storage, preparation and cooking on food; and the effect of deficiency or excess of food on the body. Nutrition in this context is broad-based, applying all the complex areas of science to the human situation.

Food can be defined as any substance, either solid or liquid, which can be consumed and utilized by the body for sustenance. Food is essential to maintain life and is basically made up of many different chemicals which react together to form **nutrients**. Nutrients are the substances which help in the growth, maintenance and reproduction of the body; they also provide the body with energy. The majority of the different foods we eat contain a mixture of various nutrients. There are five main nutrients in our food: **proteins**, **fats**, **carbohydrates**, **vitamins** and **minerals**, as well as **water**, which is essential for the body's well-being.

Energy is essential for the successful working of the body. A number of nutrients can help supply the necessary energy required for bodily processes to function efficiently and to enjoy physical activities. This energy is measured using **kilocalories** (often abbreviated to **calories**) or by the metric measurement of **kilojoules**. A kilocalorie is defined as the amount of heat required to raise 1 kg of water 1 °C (one kilocalorie is equal to 4.2 kilojoules). We often refer to the calorie content of our diet and it is important to realize that calories are not nutrients but simply a method of measuring the energy content of food (see Table 2.1).

Diet is a term which is often misused. We talk about 'following a diet' or 'going on a diet' when we want to lose weight. In fact the term 'diet' refers to the food we eat and the choices of meals we make. Each of us has a diet – what you choose for breakfast, lunch and dinner comprises your daily diet. It may vary from day to day in the different foods you choose to eat and it could well be similar to the diet of other people, especially other members of your family, but it is still your own personal diet.

A **special diet** on the other hand is where the normal diet has had to be modified in some way to help in the treatment of a medical condition. A diabetic or someone suffering from coeliac disease would have to follow a special diet as part of their medical treatment. A weight reduction diet can also be termed a special diet when the person concerned has been advised to lose weight for medical reasons. However, the term is also used in the case of someone who is trying to lose weight for cosmetic reasons as they are still having to modify their normal diet. It is debatable whether a vegetarian or vegan diet can be termed a special diet. Non-vegetarians would think so, but for those concerned it would be normal.

A **balanced diet** is one which contains sufficient amounts of the various nutrients – proteins, fats, carbohydrates, vitamins and minerals – to ensure good health. This is a rather vague definition, easy to give but difficult to apply to everyone's individual diet. We do have some help to enable us to achieve a balanced diet. The Department of Health issues guidelines on the **dietary reference values** (DRV) of nutrients our bodies require. Doctors, dietitians, nutritionists and scientists have carried out a number of research projects to determine the type of diet we should follow.

Nutritional guidelines provide information on the format we should follow to help us to achieve a healthy diet. Apart from highlighting the importance of balancing the nutrients in our diet, nutritional guidelines also build on the link between diet and health.

Not having a balanced diet can result in **malnutrition**. Malnutrition can occur when an individual is having sufficient food to maintain life but the balance of nutrients is incorrect. It is a world-wide problem and can give rise to a number of diseases such as coronary heart disease, high blood pressure and diseases of the digestive tract. Malnutrition can come in a number of forms. **Over-nutrition** can occur when an individual consumes food which contains too much of certain nutrients – such as fats and carbohydrates as in the case of obesity. **Under-nutrition** can occur when there are insufficient quantities of certain nutrients in the diet, resulting in deficiency diseases. A classic example of this is rickets (a malformation of the bones), which can occur in children, or the adult form known as osteomalacia, where the diet lacks vitamin D, calcium and phosphorus.

Starvation is a very severe state and different from malnutrition as it occurs when there is simply not enough food eaten to maintain life – there are insufficient quantities of *all* the nutrients to keep the body working properly. Unfortunately, this condition is all too common in some parts of the world, particularly in Third World countries. Although there is no starvation in Britain – indeed we are often spoilt for choice in the food available to us – malnutrition is common.

We cannot leave the subject of definitions without referring to the **measurements** which are common to nutrition. The units of measurement for energy have already been mentioned. In catering we tend to think in terms of large quantities of the various commodities, so in nutritional terms the requirements of the body for the various nutrients are very small by comparison. It is important to appreciate the terms used in nutrition when measuring various components of food (see Table 2.1). We measure the body's requirements for protein, fat and carbohydrates in terms of grams whereas vitamins and minerals are measured in milligrams and micrograms.

Table 2.1. **Metric measurements used in nutrition (accepted abbreviations are shown in brackets)**

Weight
1000 grams (g) = 1 kilogram (kg)
1000 milligrams (mg) = 1 gram (g)
1000 micrograms (μg) = 1 milligram (mg)
1000 micrograms (μgs) = 1 gram (g)
1 000 000 000 micrograms (μgs) = 1 kilogram (kg)

Volume
1000 millilitres (ml) = 1 litre (l)

Energy
1000 joules (J) = 1 kilojoule (KJ)
1000 kilojoules (KJ) = 1 megajoule (MJ)
1000 calories (c) = 1 kilocalorie (kcal)
1 kilocalorie (kcal) = 4.2 kilojoules (KJ)

Checksheet

Try to answer the following questions.

1. Define the term 'food'.

2. List the five major nutrients.

a.	*c.*	*e.*
b.	*d.*	

3. Energy is measured using k_____ and k_____.

4. Define the term 'special diet'.

5. The Department of Health issues nutrition guidelines known as the:
    a. HMI   *b.* MAFF   *c.* RDA   *d.* COMA

6. Over-nutrition is when a person eats too much food. True or false.

7. Under-nutrition is when a person is eating a diet which is low in certain nutrients. True or false.

8. How many grammes are there in 3500 mg?
    a. 35 g   *b.* 0.35 g   *c.* 3.5 g   *d.* 350 g

9. A megajoule is equivalent to:
    a. 100 KJ   *b.* 1000 KJ   *c.* 10 000 KJ   *d.* 100 000 KJ

10. How many kilojoules are equivalent to 1 kilocalorie?
    a. 2.4 KJ   *b.* 3.2 KJ   *c.* 4.2 KJ   *d.* 4.8 KJ

Now turn to the text to check your answers.

Further study

Complete the following tasks.

1. Using a special chemical balance, measure out the quantities of table salt listed below:
    a. 20 g salt (average consumption of salt per person per day)
    b. 5 g salt (the recommended amount of salt required per person per day)
    c. 1 g salt
    d. 500 mg salt
    e. 50 mg salt

    Calculate the number of milligrams in samples **a**, **b** and **c**. Then calculate the number of micrograms in all the individual samples. Note: we measure the body's requirements for vitamins and minerals in milligrams and micrograms.

2. Collect labels off ten manufactured products which give details of the nutritional content of the food on the label. For each product, list the kilocalories, then place them in order, starting with the one with the highest and going down to the one with the lowest energy content. Convert each figure into kilojoules.

three Investigating the components of food

We think of food in terms of the meals that we eat or the snacks that we consume between meals, but our minds rarely focus on the substances which make up food. In this chapter we are going to concentrate on the components of food and investigate their importance in the diet.

All living organisms consist of chemicals which react together to form larger components. Some of these larger components are termed nutrients and our bodies require these in various quantities to help with the growth, maintenance and general health of the body. Remember that at one time all the food we consume originated from a living organism whether it be a plant or an animal. In fact, we are just a bunch of chemicals produced in a very sophisticated form! Each nutrient has a particular function in the body and we shall study each in detail.

Protein

This nutrient is important as it forms the major constituent of every cell in the body.

Functions of protein in the body:

1. To help with growth.
2. For maintenance and repair.
3. To act as the basic component of hormones/enzymes.
4. As a secondary source of energy.

Growth

As proteins are the major components of body cells, the body will require a good supply as it develops from childhood to adulthood. The number of body cells increases until growth stops at around 20 years of age.

Maintenance and repair

All the cells of the body have a life-span ranging from weeks to months. These cells, with the exception of the brain cells, need to be replaced and protein is required for this purpose. Similarly if the body suffers some form of cell damage, ranging from bruising to sprains to broken bones or major surgery, healing and cell replacement will also require protein.

Basic component of hormones and enzymes

During every minute of every day, our bodies are performing thousands of different chemical reactions to aid us to live our lives. To help initiate and maintain these reactions, the body produces substances such as hormones and enzymes. These are manufactured in the body from proteins.

Secondary source of energy

The body cannot store excess protein for 'a rainy day'. So if we eat more protein foods than the body requires in a day, it has to change it to another substance that it can store or utilize. Excess protein is converted to carbohydrate or fat and either used as energy or stored as fat for use at a later time. This energy is seen as a 'secondary source' as it is *not* the main function of protein to supply energy to the body.

Proteins consist of substances known as **amino acids**. There are more than 20 different amino acids which can join together to form a protein; in fact one protein can consist of hundreds of these amino acids linked together. The arrangement or sequence of the amino acids in the protein is very important as it will determine the type of protein that is formed. To explain this more clearly, say we took six amino acids and named them A, B, C, D, E and F. Join them together and we would get:

A + B + C + D + E + F = a protein.

We could change the sequence around so that we had:

C + D + A + B + E + F = a different protein.

Again we could have:

E + A + B + C + D + F = a third type of protein.

So, although we are using the same amino acids in all three examples, because they appear in a different sequence or order each time, they produce a different type of protein. Thus the permutations of the 20 amino acids are enormous and hence the numerous different types of proteins present in our world. If we look more closely at amino acids we would find they consist of four main chemicals: carbon, hydrogen, oxygen and nitrogen. It is this last chemical which makes amino acids very difficult to store in the body, and hence the need to convert any excess to carbohydrates and fats.

Some of the amino acids are known as **essential amino acids,** so called because our bodies are unable to manufacture them from raw materials and they must therefore be supplied in our diet. Of the 20 known amino acids, 8 are essential for adults and 10 are essential for children. Proteins which contain a high percentage of essential amino acids are termed **high**

biological value proteins (HBV proteins for short). The foods which are a rich source of HBV proteins are: **meat, fish, cheese, eggs, milk** and **soya beans**. Out of this list soya beans are the only vegetable source and eggs contain the highest number of different essential amino acids. It is important to emphasize that these foods are the richest source of these essential amino acids, but amino acids can also be obtained in small quantities from other foods.

The remaining 10–12 amino acids are termed **non-essential amino acids**, not because they are unimportant but because they can be manufactured in the body if necessary and therefore do not have to be supplied in the diet on a regular basis. Proteins which contain a high percentage of the non-essential amino acids are termed **low biological value proteins** (LBV proteins for short). The foods which are a rich source of LBV proteins are: **cereals, cereal products (e.g. bread, flour-based products and breakfast cereals), pulses, nuts, seeds** and **potatoes**. All these foods are from plant sources.

It is important to realize that all the foods which are termed LBV are just as essential in the diet as those which are HBV; indeed, the body requires a good mixture of all the amino acids. If the diet supplies the non-essential amino acids, it saves the body the time and trouble of having to manufacture them.

A healthy diet will consist of a good mixture of all the various protein foods to provide as many of the essential and non-essential amino acids as possible. Such a mixture is termed **complementation of proteins**, where one food will provide the amino acids lacking in another. In this country our traditional meals tend to encourage this mixture: think, for example, of cheese on toast, Yorkshire pudding, fish and chips, macaroni cheese, toad-in-the-hole, meat and rice dishes, pasta dishes with meat or cheese, custards, and rice pudding. This method of complementary proteins is also economically sound. The HBV proteins are the most costly items in our diet, so mixing them with the less expensive LBV proteins will help any budget.

Carbohydrates

This nutrient is formed by plants in a process known as photosynthesis, where water and carbon dioxide are fused together in the presence of sunlight to form simple sugars and oxygen. Basically carbohydrates consist of three main chemicals: carbon, hydrogen and oxygen.

Functions of carbohydrate in the body:

1. Provide energy.
2. Maintain a healthy gut.

Energy

Every cell of our body requires energy to function, and this is provided by carbohydrates in the form of the simple sugar glucose. The cells utilize glucose to supply the energy they need to perform complex chemical reactions. For example, the muscle cells require energy to help with contraction and relaxation of the muscles, thus helping us to perform physical movements.

Maintaining a healthy gut

Some carbohydrates aid the passage of food through our gut, particularly the waste products after digestion and absorption. This will be explained in greater detail later in the chapter.

Carbohydrates can be subdivided into three main groups: sugars, starch, and dietary fibre.

Sugars

These can best be described as the simplest form of carbohydrates. The word 'sugar' conjures up images of spoonfuls of the white crystals we use for sweetening all types of foods. In fact this is just one of a group of sugars. The main sugars are:

Sucrose
This is the correct name for the white crystals mentioned above and can be found in many fruits and vegetables but particularly in sugar cane and sugar beet. The refined sugar is extensively used as a sweetener in our foods and is the main ingredient of **sweets, chocolates, jams, preserves** and **fizzy drinks**. It is also added to **cakes** and **biscuits** in the manufacturing process.

Maltose
This is the sugar present in all **cereal grains**. It is less sweet than sucrose but it is the sugar we use in the production of **beer**.

Lactose
This is better known as the milk sugar as it is present in varying concentrations in **milk** produced by lactating animals.

These three sugars are known as disaccharides (meaning 'two sugars'), and are formed from very simple sugars known as monosaccharides (meaning 'one sugar'). These simple sugars are **glucose, fructose** and **galactose**, which are found in some foods but on the whole they occur naturally, joined together to form the three main sugars described above. The relationship between them is shown in Table 3.1. All sugars dissolve very easily in liquids and are readily digested by the body.

Table 3.1. **The composition of sugars**

Sugars	Component simple sugars
Sucrose	1 unit of glucose + 1 unit of fructose
Maltose	2 units of glucose joined together
Lactose	1 unit of glucose + 1 unit of galactose

Starch

This is a much larger substance in chemical terms than sugars. It is composed of two substances known as **amylose** and **amylopectin**, which themselves consist of large numbers of the simple sugar glucose. Starch is referred to as a polysaccharide (meaning 'many sugars'). Unlike sugars, starch does not dissolve in liquids and is much easier to digest if cooked. It is found naturally in a number of foods, especially **cereals** and **cereal products**, and **root vegetables** such as **potatoes**. Animal products such as meat and dairy products do not contain starch.

Dietary fibre

This consists of three main substances: **cellulose**, **pectin** and **lignin**. It is also referred to as a **polysaccharide**. Unlike the other two carbohydrates already described, dietary fibre cannot be digested by the human body. It is best defined as the undigested parts of leaves, stems, roots, seeds and fruits of plants. The best sources of dietary fibre are all varieties of **fruits, vegetables, nuts** and products made from **wholegrain cereals**. The last food source can be defined as those products which are made from the whole cereal grain. Meat, fish and dairy products contain *no* dietary fibre.

Although dietary fibre cannot be digested and absorbed by the body or supply us with energy like sugars and starch, it still has an important role to play in our diet. Amazingly enough, this function has only been fully realized in recent years. Previously it was thought that if a food substance was not digested and absorbed into the bloodstream it was of little use to us, but we could not have been more wrong. The function of dietary fibre can best be summed up as follows:

1. It aids the action of the bowels and prevents constipation. It achieves this by adding bulk to the diet so that after the other nutrients have been digested and absorbed, the dietary fibre will increase the quantity of waste material entering the bowel. This will keep the bowel active and stimulate the regular movement of waste products through the length of the bowel.

2. It promotes a better control of conditions such as diabetes by slowing down the rate at which the nutrients are absorbed across the gut wall. This enables the body mechanisms to process the influx of nutrients more efficiently.

3. It helps to prevent and control overweight. By adding more bulk to the diet, dietary fibre can help to satisfy the appetite by providing that 'full' feeling we experience after eating a meal.

Research into the effects of a diet rich in dietary fibre is still being investigated and further useful functions will no doubt be uncovered. Dietary fibre and its implications for our health will be further explored in a later chapter.

Fats

These nutrients are also known as **lipids** and the term refers to the fats and oils we use in cooking as well as those present in many of our foods. Fats are solid at room temperature whereas oils are liquid, but their composition is similar.

Functions of dietary fats in the body:

1. To act as a primary source of energy.

2. To help maintain body temperature.

3. To protect vital organs.

4. To aid cell structure.

Energy

Like carbohydrates, fats supply the body with the energy it requires to function and perform physical activities. However, fats are capable of providing twice as much energy as sugars and starches.

Maintenance of body temperature

Some of the energy produced by fats is used to maintain our internal temperature at 37 °C. This is a relatively high temperature when you consider an average British summer and the fact that we like to heat our homes at around 22 °C in the winter. However, whatever the temperature outside, our bodies must always have an internal temperature of 37 °C to function properly and fats will provide the energy to achieve this. Fats also act as an insulator to prevent heat loss from the body. All of us have a layer of fat cells (adipose tissue) which covers our bodies. Some areas have thicker layers than others – the torso has quite thick layers of fat cells whereas the head, hands and feet have very little. These fatty tissues act as an insulating layer to the body.

Protection of vital organs

Layers of fat cells (adipose tissue) can also act as a buffer to protect some of our vital organs. One of the most vulnerable of these organs is the kidneys. Unlike the heart and lungs, the kidneys cannot rely on a bony structure like the rib-cage to give added protection. The kidneys are wrapped in a thick envelope of fat which will provide some protection against injury.

Aid to cell structure

The body is capable of making a number of substances from the dietary fat present in our food. One of these substances is **cholesterol**, which is present in every cell of the body to provide structure to the cell.

Fats are composed of substances known as **triglycerides**, which in turn consist of **glycerol and fatty acids**. These are mixtures of three chemicals – carbon, hydrogen and oxygen. Each triglyceride is made up of one unit of glycerol and three units of fatty acids. It is the fatty acids which give the fat/oil its properties and flavour. There are over 25 different fatty acids found in food, many of which the body can in fact make from various raw materials available. However, like some amino acids, there are a few fatty acids which must be supplied in food as the body cannot manufacture them. These are known as **essential fatty acids** or EFAs.

Fatty acids can be divided into two main groups: **saturated** and **unsaturated fatty acids**. The difference between them is the number of hydrogen atoms which are present in each type of fatty acid. A saturated fatty acid is one which has as many hydrogen atoms as it can take – in other words it is literally saturated with hydrogen. An unsaturated fatty acid, on the other hand, is one which could contain more hydrogen atoms and therefore has some 'spare places'. Unsaturated fatty acids can further divide into two groups – **monounsaturated** and **polyunsaturated fatty acids**. The difference between these lies in the number of 'spare places' the fatty acid has for more hydrogen. Monounsaturated fatty acids have one 'spare place' and could take up one more hydrogen atom, whereas polyunsaturated fatty acids have two or more 'spare places' for hydrogen atoms.

Perhaps the following analogy will help make this clearer. Take a train with a number of coaches. The first coach has no spare places as passengers have occupied every seat (saturated); the second coach has one spare seat, the rest being taken by passengers (monounsaturated) and the third coach is only half full with plenty of spare seats (polyunsaturated)!

Saturated fatty acids are found in animal fats such as **butter, lard, dripping, suet, visible fat on meats and in whole milk, cream** and **egg yolks. Margarine**, although not an animal fat, contains saturated fatty acids. One of the characteristics of most of these fats is that they are solid at room temperature and we term them hard fats. For example, one of the hardest of these fats is suet, which, unlike many fats, can be grated. This property

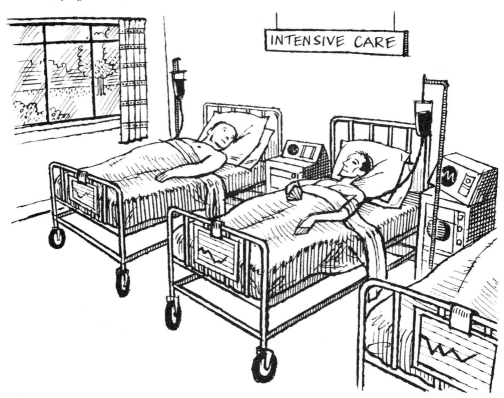

is due to the type of saturated fatty acid present in the fat, in this case a fatty acid called **stearic acid**.

Unsaturated fatty acids are found in the **vegetable oils extracted from plant seeds and nuts** and also in **oily fish** such as **trout**, **salmon**, **sardines**, **herrings** and **mackerel**. These fats are all liquid at room temperature. An example of an oil which is rich in monounsaturated fatty acids is **olive oil**, whereas those containing polyunsaturated fatty acids include **corn oil**, **rapeseed oil**, **sunflower oil**, **soya bean oil** and **oily fish**.

It is possible to change both mono- and polyunsaturated fatty acids into saturated fatty acids by introducing hydrogen into the 'spare places' (although this process is irreversible). The process is used in the manufacture of margarine, where hydrogen is bubbled through vegetable oils under pressure: this is known as **hydrogenation**. The rate at which hydrogen is introduced will depend on the type of margarine required. For a block margarine, virtually all the fatty acids present in the oil will be saturated, whereas for a spreading margarine only partial saturation needs to take place. The implications of this are that, despite the impression given in advertisements, there is no such product as a margarine which is high in polyunsaturated fatty acids – such a product would still be an oil!

At the present time there is considerable concern over the relationship between dietary fats and heart disease, not to mention the link between excessive fat intake and overweight. This is a very important topic which will be examined in detail in Chapter 8; at this stage we are merely looking at the composition of the foods we eat.

Foods containing fats/oils are also termed **visible** or **invisible** sources of fat. Visible sources would be **butter, margarine, lard, dripping, suet, white fat on meats, cream and vegetable oils**, in fact any food which is visibly fatty. Invisible fat sources would be **cakes, pastries, fried foods, biscuits, chocolate, oily fish, whole milk and cheese** – any food which has a high fat content but does not look like a fat/oil.

Vitamins

These are much smaller components of our food than the proteins, carbohydrates and fats already described.

> Functions in the body:
>
> **1.** To help to regulate the growth and repair of the body.
> **2.** To control the functioning of the body cells.

There are 13 vitamins known to be required by the body and each of these has specific functions to perform. Tables 3.2 and 3.3 list the important vitamins, giving details of their functions and the main food sources for each. Before the 1950s illnesses attributed to a lack of vitamins were common in this country. However, in our more affluent society where food is more plentiful, these deficiency diseases are much rarer. Unfortunately, in other parts of the world these conditions are still common, and information on the lack of certain vitamins is given in the tables.

Vitamins consist of organic compounds (based on the element carbon) which are required by the body in minute quantities. The chemical composition of each vitamin is very different but scientists are now able to reconstruct many vitamins synthetically in the laboratory. Vitamins are important, not just by reason of their function, but because the body cannot make a large proportion of them from other raw materials.

A short history is required at this point to clarify the naming of the vitamins. As nutrients go, their discovery as chemical compounds is relatively recent. Vitamin A, for example, was discovered in 1913 by scientists in the United States and given a letter as identification. As subsequent vitamins were discovered, they too were designated by a letter – B, C, D and so on. After a number of years it became clear that vitamin B actually consisted of two factors, so they were given the labels of B1 and B2. Further research showed that there were a number of vitamins with similar properties and functions to B1 and B2; these were therefore given the B prefix, and the B complex of vitamins was formed. Since the 1960s, when the chemical formula of each vitamin was discovered, they have been given names which fit their composition and the letters are not so frequently used. Only B12 is still waiting for a more scientific title. Names as well as letters are used for the vitamins in Tables 3.2 and 3.3.

Vitamins are classified into two main groups – **fat soluble** and **water soluble**. We will look more closely at each group.

Fat soluble vitamins

As the term indicates, these vitamins dissolve only in fat and other organic solvents. They are found in fatty foods and fat is needed to help their absorption into the body. Because they can dissolve in fat, they can be stored in the body, both in the liver and in fatty tissue (adipose tissue). Therefore it is not necessary to include these vitamins in the diet on a daily basis. The vitamins which form this group are as follows:

Vitamin A (retinol)
Vitamin D (calciferol)
Vitamin E (tocopherols)
Vitamin K (naphthoquinones)

Information on the functions and dietary sources of each of these vitamins and the diseases which can result from a deficient intake is listed in Table 3.2. There are a few additional points which are worth making.

The body is capable of manufacturing vitamin A from a substance known as **carotene**. This is the red, yellow or orange colouring found in many fruits and vegetables such as carrots, tomatoes, peaches, apricots and oranges. Carotene is *not* vitamin A but is known as its **precursor**.

Vitamin D can also be manufactured in the body. The ultraviolet rays from the sun change a substance present in our skin into vitamin D. (It is important to note that vitamin D is *not* present in the sun rays and we do *not* absorb it through our skin – a misconceived idea!) In some parts of the world this is a very important way of producing the vitamin but in this country we still rely heavily on the dietary sources of vitamin D for the obvious reason that our exposure to the sun's rays is limited. However, this vitamin is often known as the 'sunshine vitamin'.

Both vitamins A and D are added by law to all margarines manufactured in this country. This stems from a decision made by Parliament during the Second World War when food was rationed and margarine was more accessible than butter, which naturally contains these vitamins, and this law still stands today.

Table 3.2. **Fat soluble vitamins**

Vitamin	Chief dietary sources	Functions	Deficiencies
Vitamin A Preformed vitamin A (retinol)	Liver, kidney, butter, cheese, margarine, eggs.	Required for vision in dim light.	Night blindness and dried up skin, eyes and body linings.
Carotene	Carrots, green leafy vegetables, tomatoes, apricots.	Required to keep skin and body linings moist and healthy.	
Vitamin D (Cholecalciferol)	Oily fish, e.g. herrings, salmon and sardines, margarine. Some brands of yogurt and breakfast cereals are fortified with vitamin D.	Required for normal formation of bones and teeth. It promotes absorption of calcium and phosphorus.	Rickets – soft bones which bend and break easily.
Vitamin E (Group name for tocopherols and tocotrienols)	Richest source – vegetable oils, wheat germ, but contained in most foods – cereal, fish, fruit and vegetables, eggs, offal.	Relatively unknown but thought important in maintaining cell structure and red blood cells.	Deficiency is rare – can occur in premature infants causing anaemia and mild muscular dystrophy. Possible cause of low blood levels in adults.
Vitamin K	Vegetables, liver. Richest sources – cabbage, sprouts, cauliflower and spinach.	Required for formation of proteins – responsible for clotting of blood.	Prolonged bleeding – can lead to death.

Vitamins E and K are required in very small quantities and are found in a large number of foods. The main function vitamin E plays in our bodies is still uncertain – we obviously need it but are not sure why. The same is true of vitamin K although we do know that it is important for the blood to clot properly.

Can we have too much of these fat soluble vitamins? Yes, it is possible, and the result can be an enlargement and malfunction of the liver. As the body can store them, it is not necessary to have foods rich in these vitamins on a daily basis or take supplements in tablet form.

Water soluble vitamins

As the name suggests, these vitamins are soluble in water and are found in foods with a high water content. We also have a high water content, which makes storing these vitamins extremely difficult. They should therefore be present in our diet on a daily basis. They can also be lost in cooking, something we shall discuss later. The vitamins which are included in this group are:

Vitamin B complex

    thiamin B1
    riboflavin B2
    niacin (nicotinic acid)
    pyridoxin B6
    B12
    folic acid
    panthothenic acid
    biotin

Vitamin C (ascorbic acid)

The function of each of these vitamins, along with dietary sources and deficiency diseases, are listed in Table 3.3. It is worth highlighting one important fact about vitamin B12 – it can only be found in animal products. This is very important when catering for people following a vegan diet which excludes these. Niacin is the only water soluble vitamin which the body can manufacture. It can be made in the body from an essential amino acid called **tryptophan**, which is found in the HBV proteins. Vitamin C is also found in a restricted group of foods, namely fruit and vegetables, but if some of these are taken daily no problems arise.

Table 3.3. **Water soluble vitamins**

Vitamin	Chief dietary sources	Functions	Deficiencies
B group B1 Thiamin	Wholegrain cereals, nuts, pulses, meat (especially pork), bread.	Release of energy from carbohydrates.	Beri-beri – nerve disorder resulting in paralysis and muscular weakness.

B2 Riboflavin	Liver, kidney, cheese, eggs, pulses, fish, wheatgerm, milk.	Release of energy from food.	Sore skin, cracked lips, inflammation of eyes.
Nicotinic acid (Niacin)	Liver, kidney, meat, fish, wholemeal cereals, pulses.	Release of energy from food.	Pellagra – diarrhoea, dermatitis, mental disorders.
B6 Pyridoxin	Occurs widely in food especially meats, fish, eggs, wholegrain cereals and green vegetables.	In metabolism of amino acids and conversion of tryptophan to nicotinic acid. Also necessary for formation of haemoglobin.	In adults – ?anaemia, skin disorder. In children – ?convulsions.
B12	Only found in animal products. Rich sources – liver, eggs, cheese, milk, meat, fish.	Required by cells in bone marrow which form blood.	Pernicious anaemia and degeneration of nerve cells. Vegans are most susceptible.
Folic acid	Occurs in many foods but rich in offal and *raw* green leafy vegetables. Pulses, bread, oranges, bananas are good sources.	Required with B12 by cells in bone marrow which form blood.	Megaloblastic anaemia (different from pernicious): occurs among the elderly, pregnant women, and premature infants on a poor diet.
Pantothenic acid (pantolhenate)	Widespread in food, especially animal products.	Release of energy from fat and carbohydrate.	Rare, but symptoms include headache, fatigue, irritability, stomach cramps, pins and needles in feet.
Biotin	Rich sources – offal, egg yolk. Also found in milk, dairy products, cereals, fish, fruit, and vegetables.	Metabolism of fat and many vital body processes.	Adult deficiency unknown.
Vitamin C (Ascorbic acid)	Oranges, blackcurrants, dark-green leafy vegetables, peppers, new potatoes.	Required to make connective tissues and for healing wounds.	Scurvy – bleeding gums and bleeding under the skin. Wounds fail to heal.

It is unlikely that the body will ever suffer from excesses of the B complex of vitamins or vitamin C, because the body is unable to store them. If we have too many they just pass into the urine and out of the body. As long as an individual is having a variety of different foods in their diet and eating regularly, there is no need for any vitamin supplements in the form of tablets – the money spent is literally going down the drain.

Although our knowledge of the composition of vitamins is almost complete, we still have a long way to go before we fully understand the complex function they perform in our bodies. With the ever-increasing sophistication in technology, future research in this subject could revolutionize our ideas on their importance to our health.

Minerals

The body requires at least 18 minerals to help it function properly and on the whole these have many food sources.

They have a number of functions in the body which can be summed up as follows:

1. They are the major constituents of bones and teeth (calcium, phosphorus, magnesium and fluorine).

2. They control the composition of fluid levels in the body (sodium, chlorine and potassium).

3. They help the activity of a large number of enzymes and proteins which are necessary for the release and use of energy (iron, iodine, zinc and copper).

Minerals are very small substances which consist of single elements. Because they are not derived from carbon they are termed inorganic substances. A list of the main minerals, with details of their function to the body, the main dietary sources and the results of deficiencies and excesses, is given in Tables 3.4 and 3.5.

There are two main groups of minerals, **major minerals** and **trace elements**, and which group a mineral belongs to depends on the amount required by the body.

Major minerals

This group contains eight minerals, all of which are found in the body in comparatively large quantities. These minerals are **iron, calcium, phosphorus, sodium, potassium, chlorine, magnesium** and **sulphur**. Table 3.4 lists the main minerals in this group giving the food sources, functions

Table 3.4. **Major minerals**

Mineral	Sources	Functions	Deficiencies	Excesses
Iron	Red meats (lamb, beef), offal, cereal products.	Aids in the transport and utilization of oxygen in the body. Keeps blood healthy.	Anaemia.	Body does not absorb from the diet.
Calcium and phosphorus	Milk, cheese and yogurt, eggs.	Provides strong bones and teeth.	Rickets and osteomalacia.	Excreted from the body but can be deposited in the body, e.g. kidney stones.
Sodium	Milk, meat, eggs, fish naturally contain salt. Main sources: smoked fish, ham, bacon, manufactured foods.	Maintains fluid balance in the body – fluids which bathe the cells.	Rare – causes heart failure, muscular cramp.	Risk of high blood pressure.
Potassium	Vegetables, fruit, coffee, yeast extract.	Maintains fluid levels in the body – fluids inside cells.	Rare – causes heart failure.	Incorrect body fluid balance.
Chlorine	Salt, smoked fish, ham, bacon, manufactured foods.	Maintains fluid levels in the body associated with sodium.	Rare – probable cause of heart failure.	Risk of high blood pressure.
Magnesium	Wholegrain cereals, wholemeal bread, nuts, spinach. Found in many foods.	Present in the bones. Maintains the structure of cells. Co-factor for many enzymes.	Rare – can result in lethargy, irritation, depression, fits, heart attacks.	Not harmful as it is not absorbed.
Sulphur	Protein foods: meat, fish, eggs, milk.	Part of the essential amino acids – methionine and cystine – needed for growth and repair.	Probable cause of poor growth.	Excreted via the kidneys. Probably toxic to the body.

and the effects of deficiencies and excesses of each. However, although these minerals are essential in our diet, we are talking about very small absolute quantities – our needs are measured in milligrams. This does not, however, diminish their importance.

Iron

This is probably the most well known of this group and it might come as a surprise to some that vegetables, especially dark-green vegetables, are no longer listed as good dietary sources of iron. It has been discovered that although iron is richly found in these foods, it is poorly absorbed by the body due to the action of a substance known as **phytic acid**. This binds with the iron and other minerals, stopping absorption. In fact, our best food source of iron is **red meats – beef, lamb** and **pork** – and **offal**. The iron contained in these foods is readily absorbed. Other reasonable sources are **egg yolks, pulses, cereals** and **cereal products**. Those at risk from a lack of iron are likely to be women who are vegetarians or vegans. One substance which enhances iron absorption is **vitamin C** – so including foods rich in this vitamin in a diet will help. Interestingly, the body will only absorb iron from the diet when stocks are getting low and it can absorb it more efficiently from food rather than from tablets.

Calcium

This mineral has recently hit the headlines because of its link with a bone disease known as **osteoporosis**. Research is suggesting an increase in calcium intake in middle-aged and elderly women would help prevent this common complaint. Vitamin D helps in the absorption of calcium and fortunately they are found together in some foods, for instance **milk** and **cheese**. It is known that some calcium is absorbed by the body from drinking water in hard-water areas.

Sodium

This has also acquired notoriety in recent years as doctors have linked excessive intakes with high blood pressure and heart disease. This subject will be discussed at length in a later chapter; it is sufficient to note here that our intake of sodium and chlorine has rapidly increased in the past two decades as we use more convenience foods (it does not only come as table salt). Sodium, like chlorine and potassium, plays a very important role in our bodies. They help balance the fluid levels in the body and, at the risk of appearing flippant, prevent us from accumulating fluid in our limbs due to gravity or even drowning in our own fluids – a sobering thought!

Trace elements

The minerals in this category are those which are required in minute quantities (micrograms) by the body but are essential for life. There are ten trace elements: **chromium, cobalt, copper, fluorine, iodine, manganese, molybdenum, selenium, vanadium** and **zinc**. Nickel, silicon and tin are also thought to play a part in the body's utilization of food (metabolism). A list of the more commonly known trace elements can be found in Table 3.5

Table 3.5. **Trace elements**

Mineral	Sources	Functions	Deficiencies	Excesses
Chromium	Found in many foods and especially fresh vegetables, wholegrain cereals.	Known to enhance the action of enzyme insulin.	Not thought to cause diabetes but produces similar symptoms.	Not known.
Cobalt	Present in plants.	Linked with vitamin B12.	Not known.	Can cause heart failure.
Copper	Liver, shellfish, cocoa, malted milk drinks, wheat germ.	Necessary for growth of children and production of some enzymes.	In children failure to thrive, diarrhoea, anaemia.	Diarrhoea and liver damage.
Fluorine	Water, tea, seafood.	Increases resistance to tooth decay.	?Dental caries.	Mottling of teeth, bone changes.
Iodine	Seafood, salt.	Main constituent of thyroxine produced by the thyroid.	Goitre.	Rare – body does not absorb it.
Manganese	Found in many foods especially wholegrain cereals, nuts, tea.	Co-factor for several enzymes.	No known disorder.	May affect iron absorption.
Molybdenum	Vegetables particularly leaf and pulse vegetables.	Needed for several enzymes.	Probable tooth decay in children.	Symptoms similar to gout.
Selenium	Present in vegetables.	Important in cell structure.	No known disease in humans.	Toxic – could cause tooth decay.
Vanadium	Uncertain but thought to be present in many foods.	Not fully known – present in blood fats.	Not known.	Not known.
Zinc	Present in a wide variety of foods but especially milk, meat, fish.	Essential for the action of enzymes involved in growth and repair.	Stunts growth and healing is impaired.	Very large intakes are toxic – severe vomiting.

along with their dietary sources, functions and the results of deficiencies and excesses.

The exact function of these minerals in the body is not yet fully appreciated although it is known that they are involved in hormone and enzyme activity. They are all found in a wide variety of foods and as we require them in such small quantities the likelihood of any deficiency is rare if we eat a balanced diet. It is possible to have too much of these minerals and this can lead to poisoning. For example, an excess of copper will cause diarrhoea and liver damage; an excess of zinc can cause copper deficiency and in extreme cases outbreaks of vomiting. Taking supplements of any trace element can prove a very dangerous practice and requires medical supervision. Some local authorities have added controlled quantities of fluorine to drinking water to help prevent tooth decay. Fluorine has also been added to toothpaste.

Minerals, like the vitamins discussed above, are very important to our bodies but we do not fully understand their contribution to our overall well-being. Future research into the activity of minerals in the body will no doubt enlighten us further.

Water

Water is the very essence of life, and without it we could not exist. Strictly speaking it is not a nutrient, but so important is it to our lives and so abundantly found in our foods that it warrants a place in this chapter.

'Humans do not live in water; they carry their "oceans" with them' – so said William Scheider, an American professor. Over 60 per cent of our body weight is attributed to water, the majority of which is held inside the body cells with approximately 3 litres in our blood and lymph systems. The body fluids bathe the cells, maintaining the correct environment for them to function. Sodium, chlorine and potassium help to maintain the balance of fluids throughout the body, and the kidneys regulate our daily needs.

Functions of water in the body:

1. To act as a solvent and transport system – nutrients, enzymes, hormones are dissolved in fluid while oxygen and nutrients are transported to all cells in the body.

2. To aid removal of waste products which could poison the body.

3. To help to dissipate heat in the body via the sweat glands, thus helping to control the temperature of the body.

4. To act as a lubricant around joints, in the digestive tract and around the eyeballs.

5. To supply minerals in the diet in hard-water areas.

We can exist for several weeks with no food but we can only last a couple of days without water. We lose water daily in the urine and faeces and from the skin and lungs. This must be replenished by drinks and by the food we eat. All living organisms contain water, so the meat, fish, dairy produce, fruit and vegetables we eat will supplement the tea, coffee and cold drinks we drink.

Excessive losses of water can result during illnesses which involve diarrhoea and vomiting. It is essential that the fluid intake is increased at this time to prevent dehydration occurring. It is estimated that we should drink **1 litre of fluid a day** to keep our bodies 'topped up' and more if we are living in hotter climates.

Checksheet

Try to answer the following questions.

Protein

1. List two functions of protein in the body.
a.   *b.*

2. How many amino acids are there?

3. Define the term 'essential amino acids'.

4. How many essential amino acids are needed for:
   a. children   *b.* adults

5. Explain the difference between high biological value and low biological value proteins.

6. List five examples of foods which are high biological and low biological value proteins.

HBV	LBV
a.	*a.*
b.	*b.*
c.	*c.*
d.	*d.*
e.	*e.*

7. Name the best vegetable protein:
   a. nuts   *b.* seeds   *c.* baked beans   *d.* soya beans.

8. List four meal examples of 'complementation of protein'.
   a.   *c.*
   b.   *d.*
   Now check your answers by looking at the text.

Carbohydrates

1. Give two functions of carbohydrate in the body.
   a.
   b.

2. State the three main groups of carbohydrates.
   a.   *b.*   *c.*

3. Name an example of:
   a. a monosaccharide
   b. a disaccharide
   c. a polysaccharide

4. State which food these sugars can be found in:
   a. sucrose
   b. maltose
   c. lactose

5. The highest percentage of carbohydrate is found in:
   a. potatoes   *b.* rice   *c.* flour   *d.* sugar.

6. Give an example of a food which is a good source of (a) starch and (b) dietary fibre for each of the following commodities:

	Starch	*Dietary fibre*
a. vegetables		
b. pasta		
c. grains		
d. cereal product		
e. breakfast cereals		
f. fruit		

Now check your answers by looking at the text.

Fats

1. List the main functions of fat in the body.

    a.

    b.

    c.

2. Fats consist of glycerol and _____ _____.

3. The terms saturated and unsaturated refer to the amount of _____ contained in the fatty acid.

4. Name a fat which contains the following:

    a. saturated fatty acid

    b. monounsaturated fatty acid

    c. polyunsaturated fatty acid

5. The term used for the manufacture of margarine is:

    a. hydrocarbons   *b.* homogenized   *c.* gelatinization

    d. hydrogenation.

6. Give two food examples for each of the following:

    a. animal fat – visible

    b. animal fat – invisible

    c. vegetable fat – visible

    d. vegetable fat – invisible

7. List six foods/dishes/meals which you consider will provide you with the highest percentage of dietary fats.

    a.   *d.*

    b.   *e.*

    c.   *f.*

Now check your answers by looking at the text.

Vitamins

1. How many vitamins are required by the body?

2. Vitamins which are fat soluble are:

    a. vitamin A & B group   *c.* vitamin C & D

    b. vitamin A & C   *d.* vitamin A & D.

3. The chemical name for vitamin A is:
    a. calciferol   *b.* ascorbic acid   *c.* retinol   *d.* thiamin.

4. What substance is the precursor of vitamin A?
    Give two food sources which contain it.
    a.   *b.*

5. Which vitamin is known as the sunshine vitamin?

6. State the main function of each of the following:
    a. vitamin A
    b. vitamin B
        thiamin
        riboflavin
        niacin
    c. vitamin C
    d. vitamin D

7. Which vitamin could be lacking in a vegan diet?

8. Fruit and vegetables are a good source of vitamin _____.

9. Name the vitamin present in reasonable amounts in the following
    foods:
    a. tomatoes   *d.* milk
    b. bread   *e.* liver
    c. sardines   *f.* broccoli.

10. The vitamins which cannot be stored by the body are:
    a. vitamin A and C   *c.* vitamin B group and C
    b. vitamin B group and D   *d.* vitamin C and D.

Now turn to the text to check your answers.

Minerals and water

1. An example of a mineral element is:
    a. calciferol   *b.* carotene   *c.* chlorine   *d.* folic acid.

2. State the function of iron in the body:

3. Give two examples of foods rich in iron:
    a.   *b.*

4. Calcium and phosphorus form the main constituents of:
    a. bones and muscles   *c.* teeth and muscles
    b. bones and teeth   *d.* teeth and cells.

5. State the function of sodium and potassium in the body:

6. An excessive amount of sodium in the diet can result in:
    a. diabetes   *b.* overweight   *c.* cramp   *d.* hypertension.

7. An old-age pensioner is suffering from a deficiency of calcium. Name two foods which would rectify the situation.
   a.   *b.*

8. Which vitamin will help the absorption of:
   a. calcium
   b. iron

9. Name the trace element added to water supplies.

10. Give two functions of water in the body.
    a.
    b.

11. How long can we survive without water?
    a. two weeks   *b.* a few days   *c.* one day   *d.* one week.

Now turn to the text to check your answers.

Further study

Complete the following tasks.

1. Write down your intake of food over the past two days (covering work days as well as recreational days). Identify all the protein foods you have eaten. Under the headings of HBV and LBV, classify the foods which fall into each category. Then list all the examples of complementation of proteins in your intake of food.

2. From the dietary intake developed for Task 1, identify the main food sources of sugars, starch and dietary fibre in your diet. State which of the groups of carbohydrate you eat the most.

3. List ten foods/dishes/meals which you consider will provide you with the highest percentage of dietary fats. How often do you eat these foods?

4. Produce a questionnaire for students in your college to determine the most popular fat/oil and fatty food that is eaten.

four

How *the body uses food*

Having investigated the components of food, we shall now go on to consider how the body copes with the food we give it. Basically, the body breaks down the food into manageable units, absorbs it into the blood system and eventually transports it to every body cell, where it is used for a number of functions. This is a very general way of describing what is in fact a very complex process involving numerous complicated chemical reactions – the body has often been compared to the eighth wonder of the world for its complexity. We cannot go too deeply into these complexities here. However, some understanding of how the body uses food is very important for nutrition.

The whole process can be divided into three main parts – digestion, absorption and utilization. Before we look further at each of these areas, we need to look briefly at the anatomy of the body. The digestive system is where the main work of breaking down food takes place and Figure 4.1 shows the names of the main sections of the system. The digestive tract itself is about 6 m long and is packed quite tightly inside us. In fact, it is a long tube straight through the middle of us similar to a doughnut with a hole! The tube varies in size and shape along its length according to the function of the particular area. For example, it broadens out to form an elasticated sack, known as the stomach, which churns and mixes the food. The whole of the digestive tract is very muscular with longitudinal, circular and diagonal muscles providing the elasticity required to move the food along its length. The environment inside the tube is very different from that inside other parts of the body: it is moist and warm and makes an ideal home for the many essential bacteria, as well as some pathogenic (disease-producing) bacteria, which make a permanent home for themselves in the bowel.

The digestion or breakdown of food into its component parts takes place along the first third of the tube and is almost complete by the time it reaches the small intestine. The nutrients are absorbed through the walls of the small intestine and the remainder of the digestive tract is used for the processing of the waste material from our food, helped along the way by the bacteria mentioned above. The length of time it takes food to pass through the digestive tract varies with the type of food we eat and the frequency of our meals, but an average time would be between 24 and 30 hours.

Digestion

Digestion is the breaking down of food to its component parts and involves

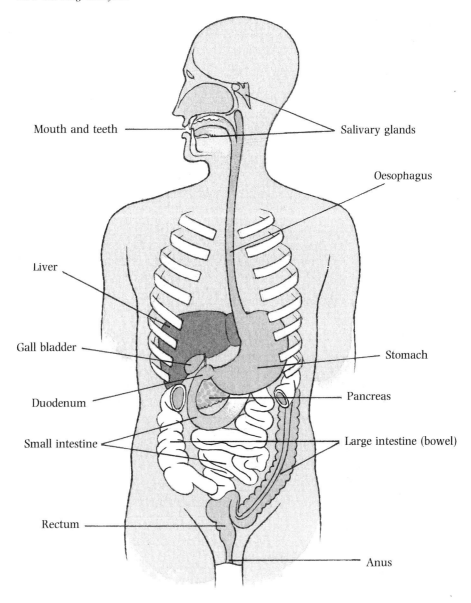

Mouth and teeth

Salivary glands

Oesophagus

Liver

Gall bladder

Duodenum

Small intestine

Rectum

Stomach

Pancreas

Large intestine (bowel)

Anus

Figure 4.1   The human digestive system

the release of nutrients to make them available to the body. The breakdown of food is achieved either by mechanical or by chemical means.

Mechanical digestion

This is the breakdown of food by physical means such as mixing, churning and grinding. It plays an important role in softening the food and mixing it with the various digestive juices and enzymes. The main areas of mechanical digestion are:

The mouth

The teeth grind the food with the help of the tongue and cheek muscles. There are 32 teeth of diverse shapes and sizes performing different types of grinding and tearing motions. The tongue and cheek muscles help mix the food, and move it continuously towards the teeth, which help break it up. When the food is suitably softened, the tongue moves it towards the back of the mouth cavity into the throat, where it is swallowed.

The stomach

The food (now known as **chyme**) is further mixed together by the actions of the many muscles which make up the stomach wall, a process which can be likened to a washing machine churning and mixing.

The digestive tract

The food passes through the digestive tract with the help of the longitudinal, circular and diagonal muscles present in the tract walls. As they contract and relax the 'food' is pushed along the tube. This movement is known as **peristalsis**.

Chemical digestion

This happens when the food is broken down with the aid of a number of chemicals (see Table 4.1). This occurs in two main ways.

With the aid of juices

These are secreted at intervals along the part of the tract involved in digestion, and they mix with the food. They are either slightly alkaline or acidic, and so help to break down the food and soften the links between the component parts of each nutrient. The main juices are as follows:

1. Salivary juice, secreted by the salivary glands into the mouth. It is slightly alkaline.

2. Gastric juice, secreted by glands in the stomach walls. It contains dilute hydrochloric acid.

3. Bile, produced by cells in the liver, passes to the gall-bladder and is released into the duodenum to act as an emulsifier to fats. Bile is slightly alkaline in property.

4. Pancreatic juice, produced by cells in the pancreas, is poured into the duodenum. It is alkaline.

5. Intestinal juice, produced by glands in the wall of the small intestine. It is alkaline.

With the aid of enzymes

These are chemicals which aid the breakdown of the 'food'. An enzyme is known as a biological catalyst which controls the chemical reactions that occur in the body. There are many different types of enzymes in the body, each with a specific job to do. They control chemical reactions by helping

Table 4.1. **The chemical breakdown of nutrients in the digestive tract**

Part of digestive tract	Name of digestive juice	Acid or alkali	Enzymes present	Action on nutrients
Mouth	Saliva	Slightly alkali	Salivary amylase	Breaks down starch to maltose.
Stomach	Gastric juice	Acid	1. Rennin 2. Pepsin	Clots milk. Breaks down proteins to peptides.
Duodenum receives juices from: (a) liver	Bile (stored in gall-bladder)	Alkali	None	Emulsifies fat.
(b) pancreas	Pancreatic juice	Alkali	1. Pancreatic amylase	Breaks down starch to maltose.
			2. Lipase	Breaks down fat to fatty acids + glycerol.
			3. Trypsin	Breaks down proteins to peptides.
Small intestine	Intestinal juice	Alkali	1. Maltase	Breaks down maltose to glucose.
			2. Sucrase	Breaks down sucrose to glucose + fructose.
			3. Lactase	Breaks down lactose to glucose + galactose.
			4. Peptidases	Breaks down peptides to amino acids.

either to speed up or to slow down the reaction, but they do not themselves get involved in the chemical reactions. There are a number of enzymes known as the digestive enzymes which help in the chemical breakdown of food. These can be divided into three main groups.

Amylases
These help in the breakdown of carbohydrates from starch to sugars.

Salivary amylase is present in salivary juice, and pancreatic amylase is present in the pancreatic juice.

Proteases
These help in the breakdown of proteins to amino acids and include pepsin and rennin, which are present in the gastric juice in the stomach, trypsin, which is present in the pancreatic juice, and the peptidases, which are present in the intestinal juice.

Lipases
These help to break down the emulsified fats to glycerol and fatty acids. Lipase is present in the pancreatic juice.

Absorption

By the time the foods we have eaten have reached the small intestine they are unrecognizable as, say, 'meat and two veg'. All the food has been softened and the majority has been broken down during digestion, releasing the nutrients and converting them into their smallest components. However, even at this stage, they are still considered to be 'outside' the body. They enter the body by passing through the walls of the small intestine into the blood system – this is known as absorption.

To speed up this process, the inside lining of the small intestine is convoluted into tiny finger-like projections called **villi**, whose purpose is to increase the surface area for absorption. Figures 4.2 and 4.3 show the inner lining of the small intestine in diagrammatic form, along with an enlargement of a single villus.

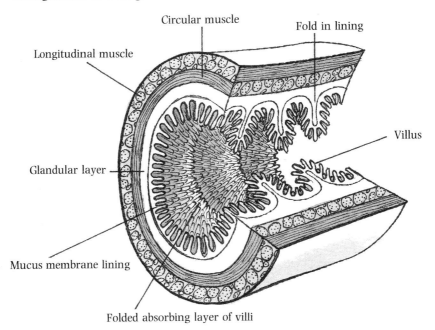

Figure 4.2   Cross-section of the small intestine

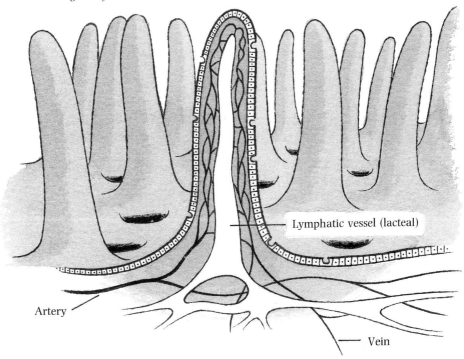

Figure 4.3   Enlargement and cross-section of the villus

Nutrients are transported through the walls of the small intestine by either passive or active means. Passive movement of the nutrients is when they slowly diffuse through the wall of the small intestine into the bloodstream, whereas active transport occurs when energy is required to assist their passage.

The water soluble nutrients such as amino acids (protein), simple sugars (carbohydrate), minerals and water soluble vitamins pass directly into the bloodstream and are carried to the liver for processing. The fatty acids and glycerol (fats), along with the fat soluble vitamins, are passed into the lymph system. Eventually the lymph system transports these substances to the blood system, which distributes them throughout the body.

The lymph forms a bridge between the blood and the cells of the body, collecting substances from the tissues and returning them to the general blood system. The lymphatic system differs from the blood system in that it is not an enclosed system, but flows in one direction only. The actions of muscles and valves cause it to move around – it is not pumped by the heart. The lymph is a fluid similar to blood plasma and flows from the tissues towards the neck, where it empties into the bloodstream.

Once the nutrients have passed through the walls of the small intestine the remaining undigested foods pass on into the large bowel. These consist mainly of dietary fibre which has been softened during digestion but not broken down. There are also large quantities of water which have been poured into the digestive tract during digestion. The main function of the large bowel is to reclaim the water by absorption and to concentrate the waste into faeces. The latter is achieved with the help of large quantities of bacteria, known as flora, which make their permanent home in the bowel. They help to break down some of the undigested substances, producing small quantities of vitamin K and the B group, especially B12. These are absorbed through the lining of the bowel and enter the blood system. The passage of substances through the bowel can take anything from one to three days depending upon the quantity of waste. The higher the quantity of dietary fibre in the daily diet the more efficient the working of the bowel becomes. Diarrhoea occurs when the lining of part of the bowel wall becomes infected and water fails to be absorbed.

Before we turn to look at the way our bodies use the nutrients supplied in our food, let us sum up the process discussed so far by asking the following question:

What happens to our food when we eat it?

Let us take each nutrient in turn.

Protein

1. It is mechanically broken down by the teeth.

2. It mixes with the gastric juice in the stomach, and the dilute hydrochloric acid, along with the enzyme pepsin, breaks it down into peptides.

3. In children the enzyme rennin helps to clot milk and break down the protein in milk.

4. In the duodenum, the enzyme trypsin present in the pancreatic juice completes the digestion by aiding the breakdown of peptides to amino acids.

5. The amino acids are then absorbed through the walls of the small intestine and enter the bloodstream.

Fats

1. They are mechanically broken down by the teeth and the action of the stomach.

2. As the fats are released into the small intestine by the stomach, the gall-bladder contracts and bile passes down the bile duct to the duodenum.

3. The bile mixes with the fats to form an emulsion – breaking down the fats to smaller globules.

4. The enzyme lipase, present in the pancreatic juice, is able to help break down the emulsion to fatty acids and glycerol.

5. The fatty acids and glycerol then pass through the walls of the small intestine into the bloodstream.

Carbohydrates

Starch

1. It is mechanically broken down by the teeth and mixed with the salivary juice containing the enzyme salivary amylase, in the mouth.

2. The enzyme helps the breakdown of starch to maltose.

3. Having passed through the stomach and entered the duodenum, any remaining starch is broken down into maltose by the enzyme pancreatic amylase present in the pancreatic juice.

4. Maltose is broken down to glucose in the small intestine by the action of the enzyme maltase present in the intestinal juice.

5. The glucose passes through the wall of the small intestine into the bloodstream.

Sugars

1. Sucrose and lactose, the sugars present in cane and beet sugar and in milk, pass along the digestive tract until they reach the small intestine.

2. Sucrose is broken down to glucose and fructose by the action of the enzyme sucrase present in the intestinal juice. The simple sugars are absorbed across the wall of the small intestine into the bloodstream.

3. Lactose is broken down to glucose and galactose by the action of lactase present in the intestinal juice. They are absorbed across the wall of the small intestine into the bloodstream.

4. Maltose, which is present in some of the foods we eat, is broken down (as in starch) to form glucose.

Dietary fibre

This is mechanically broken down by the action of the teeth and muscles, but the dietary fibre is only softened and cannot be broken down further. It adds 'bulk' to our diet so that, after the nutrients have been absorbed, there is a sufficient quantity of waste to move through the large intestine and out of the body.

Vitamins

1. Vitamins are so small that they do not have to be broken down but are simply released from food. This is achieved when food is mechanically broken down in the mouth and stomach and mixed with the juices.

2. All the vitamins pass through the wall of the small intestine and enter the blood system.

3. Vitamin C (ascorbic acid) will help the mineral iron to be absorbed, whereas vitamin D (calciferol) aids the absorption of calcium.

Minerals

1. Like vitamins, minerals are so small that all that is needed for absorption to take place is their release from food. This is achieved by the mechanical action of the teeth and stomach and by mixing with the various juices in the digestive tract.

2. The minerals are absorbed through the walls of the small intestine and enter the blood system.

3. Phytic acid, which is present in green vegetables and unprocessed bran, can bind with minerals such as iron, calcium and magnesium and prevent them from being absorbed.

Utilization

In this section we shall examine the way the body utilizes the food we eat. The description which follows is a very simple account of a highly complex process known as **metabolism**. Metabolism is the system whereby each nutrient is used in the body to help it function correctly. The nutrients are metabolized by way of the **metabolic pathways**, which are a series of step-by-step chemical reactions which take place in the cells of the body. These pathways are highly complex and the description is beyond the scope of this book, but it is important to realize that the nutrients have to proceed through a series of chemical processes once they have been absorbed through the wall of the small intestine, before they perform their individual function.

Taking each nutrient in turn we can briefly and simply describe the main processes involved.

Carbohydrates

After absorption the simple sugars – glucose, fructose and galactose – are transported in the blood to the liver. Here they are utilized in a number of ways.

1. They are transported as glucose to all the cells of the body, to be used directly for energy, via a series of steps which also produces carbon dioxide and water as a waste product.

2. They are converted into an insoluble substance called glycogen and stored in the liver and in muscle cells, ready to be used for energy when required.

3. They are converted into triglycerides (fats) and stored in the fat cells (adipose tissue) directly under the skin to act as an insulating layer and as a store of energy for when the body requires it.

Fats

After absorption, the fatty acids and glycerol are immediately rebuilt into triglycerides and carried to the bloodstream via the lymph system. The liver further changes the fats into a number of substances the body requires, for example phospholipids and cholesterol, which are important structural substances needed by every cell of the body. Some of the fats are used directly for energy while others are stored in the adipose tissue for later energy use or as protection and insulation.

Protein

After absorption through the wall of the small intestine, the amino acids are carried in the bloodstream to the liver, where they are used in a number of ways.

1. The majority of essential and non-essential amino acids are used to manufacture the proteins and enzymes required by every cell.

2. Some amino acids can be converted to other amino acids which the body may be short of and require.

3. Any excess amino acids are converted into glucose and used as energy (like carbohydrates) or formed into urea and excreted from the body via the kidneys.

Vitamins

These are transported to the liver and distributed throughout the body to assist in a number of tasks. For example many of the B group vitamins are required by each cell to aid the release of energy from carbohydrates, fats and proteins – in other words they are important in the efficient running of the metabolic pathways.

Minerals

Like the vitamins, the minerals are transported to the liver and then to various parts of the body where they have particular functions to perform or are important ingredients in the manufacture of a number of different substances – for example iron is made into haemoglobin and iodine is needed for the manufacture of thyroxine.

As will be clear from the above description, the liver plays a major role in metabolism. It is the body's factory, taking in nutrients as raw materials and producing all sorts of different substances the body requires to function properly.

A high percentage of the nutrients we consume will either provide or be involved in the production of **energy**, and so enable each cell of our body to function properly. It is therefore important that we look more closely at how our bodies utilize this energy.

We have seen that fats, carbohydrates and proteins can provide the body with potential energy. Alcohol, too, will supply some energy to the body.

The term 'potential' is used as it is known that the nutrients can supply a certain amount of energy, but the body may not always use it all. The amount of energy each nutrient is capable of producing in the body has been calculated by scientists, and is listed below.

---

1 g fat provides 37 kilojoules or 9 kilocalories.

1 g carbohydrate provides 16 kilojoules or 3.75 kilocalories.

1 g protein provides 17 kilojoules or 4 kilocalories.

1 g alcohol provides 29 kilojoules or 7 kilocalories.

So if the nutrient content of a food is known it is quite possible to calculate the potential energy that food will provide the body with. This has been achieved by scientists who have devised a set of **food tables** to help our calculations. Food tables list the energy values of food in kilojoules and kilocalories as well as giving the weight of the individual nutrients present in each food. An individual's daily energy intake can be determined by recording the weight and type of food and drink eaten and drunk over a 24-hour period and calculating the energy value from the food tables. For an accurate picture this should be repeated for several days and an average figure calculated.

Energy has been defined as the ability to do work, and every cell of the body has a job to perform and requires energy to do it. It would be an impossible task to list all these functions and show in detail how energy is used but it is feasible to group these functions under three main headings.

Maintenance of life

This is defined as the amount of energy required to maintain the body at complete rest. It is known as the **basal metabolic rate** or BMR. This is the amount of energy the body needs just to keep alive – to keep the heart beating, the lungs inflating, the digestive system working, the kidneys and many other bodily functions working. It is possible to measure the amount of energy an individual requires to maintain life by using one of two methods. The first is called **direct calorimetry** and involves measuring in kilojoules or kilocalories the amount of heat given off by the body when it is at rest – i.e. when no physical activity is being carried out. The second method is called **indirect calorimetry** and involves measuring the amount of carbon dioxide a person gives off when at rest. When this is known, it is possible to calculate the amount of oxygen a person has taken in over the same period of time while at rest. Oxygen is required to release energy in the cells and scientists know the amount of oxygen needed to release a given amount of energy. So by knowing the amount of oxygen taken in by the body, a simple mathematical calculation will give the number of kilojoules or kilocalories of energy which has been expended. A method of assessing if the BMR is high or low, often used today in hospitals, is to test the thyroid function, which will indicate how much thyroxine this gland is producing. Thyroxine is a hormone which regulates energy expenditure.

The BMR will vary from person to person depending on age, body size, body composition and whether they are male or female. The BMR will increase during childhood and then gradually decrease with age; men appear to have a higher BMR than women; a large person has a higher level than a small person and an individual with a higher percentage of lean tissue to fatty tissue will have a higher BMR than someone of the same weight but with a greater proportion of fatty tissue. It is therefore difficult to give exact figures for energy requirements for BMR but here are some indications:

> For children: 2100–4200 kilojoules (500–1000 kilocalories) per day
> For women: 5400–6300 kilojoules (1300–1500 kilocalories) per day
> For men: 6700–7500 kilojoules (1600–1800 kilocalories) per day

Physical activity

The body expends energy carrying out physical activities – any muscular movement will require energy. The more physical the activity the more energy will be required to perform it. Table 4.2 lists the average energy expenditure for a variety of activities and it can be seen that swimming, walking up stairs, squash and running fall into the category of strenuous activities. However, for us to use up large quantities of energy we must sustain these activities for some time.

We live in an age when we can call upon the services of a variety of machines to perform many of the tasks which would normally expend a lot of energy. Vacuum cleaners take the strain off brushing floors, cars stop us from having to walk and run, cement mixers do the mixing for cement – to cite just a few examples.

Special needs

There are times in our lives when our needs for energy are increased. Young children require an increase in energy to help growth. Women who are pregnant or breast-feeding their babies also require an increase in energy. An individual requires more energy after a major operation, to aid the healing process. If you are involved in competitive sports, you will expend more energy than normal. Thus more energy is required by the body to help compensate for these needs.

Table 4.2. **The average energy expenditure for a number of physical activities**

Very light under 3 kcals/ minute	Light 3–5 kcals/ minute	Moderate 5–7 kcals/ minute	Heavy 7–10 kcals/ minute	Very heavy above 10 kcals/ minute
under 180 kcals/ hour	180–300 kcals/ hour	300–450 kcals/ hour	450–600 kcals/ hour	above 600 kcals/ hour
Sleeping Sitting quietly Standing Writing Cooking at home	Military drill Most domestic work Large-scale catering Bricklaying Plastering Painting Mechanized agricultural work Driving a truck Golf	General labouring (pick and shovel) Non-mechanized agricultural work Ballroom dancing Gardening Tennis Cycling Horse riding	Coal mining (hewing and loading) Football Country dancing Disco dancing	Lumber work Furnace men (steel industry) Swimming (crawl) Cross-country running Squash Hill climbing Skiing Walking up stairs

Total energy expenditure

This is the sum of all the energy expended by the body. The daily total can be calculated by adding together the BMR, the physical activities performed by the body and any special requirements.

This chapter has examined what happens to our food when we eat it and how the body uses the nutrients we supply in our diet. The description has been purposely kept as simple as possible but it is hoped that the impression has been gained that the body is a quite remarkable machine which can perform amazing feats to help us live the lifestyles we choose.

Checksheet

Try to answer the following questions.

Digestion

1. Define the term digestion.

2. The digestive system breaks down protein to:
a. fatty acids **b.** glycerol **c.** amino acids **d.** hydrochloric acid.

3. Mechanical digestion is done by the:
   a. small intestine   *b.* teeth   *c.* enzymes   *d.* oesophagus.

4. The enzyme group involved in the digestion of starch is:
   a. proteases   *b.* amylases   *c.* lipases   *d.* rennin.

5. Fats are emulsified with the help of:
   a. enzymes   *b.* hydrochloric acid   *c.* bile   *d.* saliva.

6. The movement of food through the digestive system by muscular contractions is known as:
   a. peristalsis   *b.* osmosis   *c.* photosynthesis   *d.* dialysis.

7. The enzyme which acts on fat is:
   a. invertase   *b.* trypsin   *c.* amylase   *d.* lipase.

8. State what happens to vitamins and minerals during digestion.

9. During digestion, carbohydrates break down to _____, and fats break down to _____ and _____.

Absorption

1. Digested food is absorbed in the:
   a. large intestine   *b.* stomach   *c.* small intestine   *d.* pancreas.

2. Villi help to:
   a. enable the food to pass through quickly.
   b. increase the surface area of absorption.
   c. speed up the breakdown of food.
   d. capture food as it passes by.

3. Passive transport is:
   a. osmosis   *b.* diffusion   *c.* peristalsis   *d.* dialysis.

4. Fatty acids and glycerol are transported via the:
   a. blood   *b.* water   *c.* bile   *d.* lymph.

5. Absorption of minerals can be prevented by:
   a. vitamins   *b.* fatty acids   *c.* phytic acid   *d.* phosphorus.

6. State the main function of the large intestine.

Utilization

1. All nutrients are first transported to the:
   a. liver   *b.* pancreas   *c.* stomach   *d.* kidneys.

2. Carbohydrates are transported around the body as:
   a. glycogen   *b.* glucose   *c.* amino acids   *d.* insulin.

3. Name the nutrients which supply energy to the body.

4. How many kilojoules will 1 g of fat provide:

   a. 3 kJ   **b.** 16 kJ   **c.** 17 kJ   **d.** 29 kJ

5. Define the term basal metabolic rate.

6. List the three ways that the body uses energy.
   a.
   b.
   c.

7. Give three physical activities which expend high levels of energy.
   a.   **b.**   **c.**

8. List three physical activities which are considered to be 'light activities'.
   a.   **b.**   **c.**

Now turn to the text to check your answers.

Further study

Complete the following tasks.

1. Produce a chart to describe in detail what happens to the following meal during digestion:

> **Steak and kidney pie**
>
> **Jacket potato**
>
> **Carrots and peas**
>
> **Pear condé**

Tip: First find out which nutrients are present in the food.

2. How long does it take for food to pass through the digestive system? Enlist the help of a volunteer to eat a portion of sweetcorn and note the time of eating. Ask the volunteer to keep a careful watch and note the time it takes to pass through the system!
Note: Sweetcorn is not completely broken down in the body and kernels of sweetcorn will pass right through it.

3. Keep a diary of the main physical activities you undertake in one day, estimating the time taken for each activity. Calculate the kilojoules/kilocalories used by the body to perform these activities.

4. Keep a diary of your food intake for one day, weighing the foods eaten. Using food tables, calculate the kilojoules/kilocalories of each food. Total the day's energy intake by adding up the kilojoules/kilocalories for the day.

five

Changes to food

In the preceding two chapters, we have examined the components of food and described how the body breaks down and utilizes it. You would be forgiven for thinking that this is the end of the story, but in fact, we can alter the nutritional content of our food even before we have eaten it. In this chapter, we shall be examining how the nutrients of perishable foods are affected by various methods of storage, preparation and cooking.

The effects of storage on food

If food is stored in unsuitable conditions, then this can result in what is called **food spoilage**, when the appearance, smell and taste of food is radically altered. The nutrients can be greatly changed as the food is gradually broken down by the action of enzymes in the process of natural decay, by micro-organisms such as bacteria, moulds and yeasts, and by the loss of moisture. These changes will render the food unfit and unsuitable for human consumption.

Even if perishable foods are stored correctly – by refrigerating meat, meat products, fish, eggs, milk, cheese and other dairy produce, chilling fruits and salad vegetables, and storing vegetables in a dry, cool, well-ventilated store room away from the light – some changes in the state of the nutrients will occur.

If storage conditions are correct, proteins and carbohydrates – starch, sugars and dietary fibre – will suffer very little change. Fats and products containing fats, such as pastries and cakes, can deteriorate with time as the fats turn 'rancid', which means that some of the fats break down into their component parts of glycerol and fatty acids. The result of this process is that the flavour changes and the product becomes unacceptable to eat. Minerals do not appear to be affected by storage as long as the conditions are suitable.

Vitamins are the only other nutrient which show signs of changing during storage. Out of the two main groups of vitamins, it is the water soluble vitamins which suffer the most changes. Some of the B-complex vitamins are sensitive to light, especially ultraviolet light. For example, large quantities of riboflavin (vitamin B2) will be lost in bottled milk in a few hours if it is left in light areas and not stored in the dark. Thiamin, niacin and pantothenic acid are fairly stable during storage.

Vitamin C, which is light-sensitive, suffers most in storage as the vegetables and fruit tissues continue to use up the vitamin C manufactured during growth. So new potatoes will contain up to 30 mg of vitamin C per 100 g whereas after six months of storage the old potatoes will only contain about 10 mg per 100 g. This assumes that the potatoes are stored correctly; more will be lost if the product is damaged or bruised. With fruit and vegetables being imported from all parts of the world, there will be loss of vitamin C in transit from even good sources of the vitamin, such as grapefruit and oranges. Vitamin C appears to be 'protected' by acids so acid fruits will slow down the loss.

Fat soluble vitamins suffer minimal loss during storage, although vitamin A is sensitive to light and oxygen and is destroyed when fats turn rancid.

The effects of preparation on food

During the preparation of some perishable foods, nutrients can be lost in **wastage**. This is particularly so in the case of fruit and vegetables, where many important vitamins and minerals are stored just beneath the skin, the removal of which can reduce the nutritional content of the finished product considerably. For example, if old potatoes are peeled a high percentage of dietary fibre, as well as iron, thiamin, niacin, and vitamin C, are lost. Retaining the skin on potatoes during cooking and serving them intact, as in the case of new potatoes or baked (jacket) potatoes, will help ensure that the maximum nutritional value of the food is maintained. In Scandinavian countries, all potatoes are cooked with the skins intact and, if necessary, peeled after cooking when some dietary fibre will be lost but vitamins and minerals are retained.

Obviously there are fruits and vegetables that cannot be eaten with the peel/skin – for example bananas, grapefruit, oranges and swedes – while the outer leaves of some cabbages can be very tough and bitter. However, if root vegetables could just be washed and cut there would be obvious nutritional advantages. Some fruits will provide added colours and textures to certain dishes if the skins are retained: using a variety of different eating apples in a fruit salad, for example, can provide a pleasing mixture of skin colours, and using a red-skinned apple to decorate a *flan aux pommes* imparts colour to the finished dish as well as enhancing the fibre content!

Other perishable commodities do not suffer from too much wastage during preparation. Some fat can be lost during the preparation of some meat dishes, for example when a best-end of lamb is trimmed to expose the bones and when lean muscle is lost during the preparation of tournedos from beef fillet. Using boned meat in dishes will provide a higher percentage of available nutrients weight for weight compared with meat served on the bone.

Probably the highest nutritional loss due to wastage occurs when vegetables are subjected to various cutting methods, as illustrated in Figure 5.1. Root vegetables are mainly affected and cuts include *mirepoix*, *macédoine*, *jardinière*, *julienne*, *brunoise* and *paysanne*. The smaller the cut the higher the wastage. Turned potatoes also includes a high percentage of waste whether the cut is *cocotte*, *château* or *fondant*. The use of these cuts of vegetables will not enhance the nutritional value of a meal, and not only because of the waste incurred.

The water soluble vitamins (vitamin B-complex and vitamin C) and all minerals are particularly vulnerable during the preparation process because they easily 'leach' into any fluid and the vitamins, and some of the minerals, readily **oxidize** when in contact with air. Being water soluble means that contact with any fluid will cause the vitamins and minerals to dissolve in that fluid and be lost to the food they have 'leached' out of. Oxidizing when in contact with air means that the vitamin undergoes a chemical change when it mixes with the oxygen present in the air and becomes a different substance, and is therefore no longer of nutritional use. The oxidizing of the vitamins and minerals can occur when food such as vegetables, fruit, meat and fish is cut and its cells exposed to air. 'Leaching' can occur if prepared vegetables are stored in water prior to cooking.

For this reason, using cuts of vegetables, in particular *julienne*, *brunoise* and *paysanne* which have a very small surface area, means that the maximum amount of nutrients are exposed to the oxidation process. However, the quantity of vulnerable vitamins and minerals is not high in the root vegetables, although they do form a useful and regular supply in our diet. It is important to limit the inclusion of these cuts of vegetables while planning menus so that the overall nutritional balance is not affected.

Fine shredding of leaf vegetables such as cabbage and lettuce will also cause loss of vitamins and minerals by oxidation. Although the overall finish of the meal on the plate may be enhanced by this method, tearing the vegetables will help to retain some nutrients and is worth considering.

Storing vegetables and fruits in water prior to cooking should be avoided; if really necessary, it should be for a very limited amount of time. The practice of storing peeled potatoes in a sink of water overnight for use the next day is a nutritional disaster as all that will be left will be soggy starch! Ideally *all* vegetables should be prepared just prior to cooking. Whereas this can easily be achieved in the home, it is very difficult when catering for large numbers. But careful planning of work schedules can minimize the length of time necessary for such storage.

The effects of cooking on food

That perishable foods go through considerable changes during the cooking process is obvious. Modifications in colour, texture, structure and taste occur with most foods. The fate of the nutrients is closely linked with these changes and some can be altered and destroyed completely. It will be easier to explain these changes if we look at each of the nutrients individually.

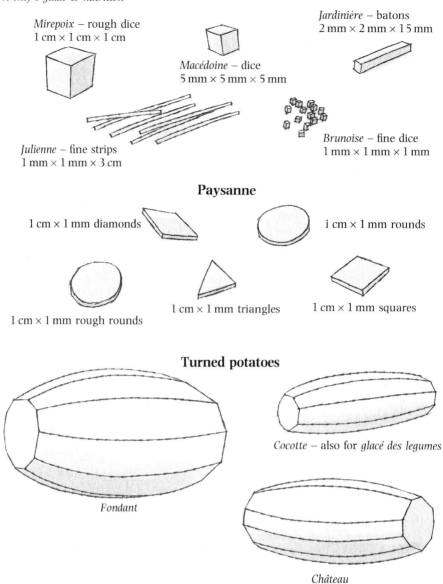

Mirepoix – rough dice
1 cm × 1 cm × 1 cm

Macédoine – dice
5 mm × 5 mm × 5 mm

Jardinière – batons
2 mm × 2 mm × 15 mm

Julienne – fine strips
1 mm × 1 mm × 3 cm

Brunoise – fine dice
1 mm × 1 mm × 1 mm

Paysanne

1 cm × 1 mm diamonds

i cm × 1 mm rounds

1 cm × 1 mm rough rounds

1 cm × 1 mm triangles

1 cm × 1 mm squares

Turned potatoes

Cocotte – also for *glacé des legumes*

Fondant

Château

Figure 5.1   Cuts of vegetables

Proteins

Cooking methods will not destroy proteins but they can toughen them to such an extent that it is very difficult for the body to digest them. When heated, proteins change their chemical structure. This change is irreversible and is termed **denaturation**. As heating continues the proteins coagulate or set, and if overcooked they toughen, shrink and become less digestible. All methods of cooking will cause these changes but some more quickly than others. For example, dry methods of cooking such as grilling and baking will cause protein in meat to denature and coagulate quickly, squeezing out juices containing the vitamin B group and minerals – a process known as **syneresis**. Moist methods of cooking will have the same effect but take much longer to achieve. 'Well done' meat will be much harder for the body to digest than meat just cooked through; a hard-boiled egg is more difficult to digest than a soft-boiled egg.

Carbohydrates

These include sugar, starch and dietary fibre.

Sugar

This is not easily destroyed by cooking. Dry heat – such as grilling a sugar topping on a *crème brûlée* – will cause the sugar to melt and quickly **caramelize**, producing a brown, clear, brittle toffee. If heating continues, the mixture will burn leaving a black, carbon residue. With moist heat, the sugars will dissolve into the liquid, forming a syrup which gradually caramelizes after the mixture has passed boiling point. The syrup becomes more viscous (thicker) as the liquid evaporates. Continued heating will result in the mixture burning and forming a carbonized residue. Providing food is not over-cooked, sugar is not easily destroyed but just changes its consistency and flavour.

Starch

This becomes more digestible with cooking and easier for the body to cope with. Dry heat causes starch to change to a brown colour, forming a sugar called **dextrin**. This process is known as **dextrinization** and occurs, for example, when bread is toasted. Moist heat will help the starch soften and become more digestible. When starch is added to a liquid and heated, as in the making of a roux-based sauce, the starch grains soften and start to absorb the liquid. The starch grains swell and finally burst, thickening the mixture. This process is known as **gelatinization** and makes the starch much more digestible.

Dietary fibre

This will be softened by moist cooking methods such as boiling, poaching and steaming, and made more palatable. However, no amount, or method, of cooking will enable us to digest the fibre.

Fats

These can be destroyed by excess heat in cooking. When a fat starts to give off a blue haze when heated, molecules of fat are breaking down into their component parts of fatty acids and glycerol. This is known as the smoke point. Solid fats have a much lower smoke point than oils and butter, which, as it is not a pure fat, will break down at a lower temperature than a pure fat such as lard will. Foods cooked in fats and oils which are above their smoke point will tend to burn, but they will also taste bitter as a result of the breakdown of the fat. Fats are more easily absorbed when they are heated. So foods which are shallow- or deep-fat fried will readily increase their fat content by absorption.

Minerals

Little is known about the effect of cooking methods on the minerals present in food. However, it is known that some, especially iron, leach out of food during cooking, especially if moist methods are used. Whether heat destroys or changes some of the minerals is not fully known, but on the whole it would appear to have little effect. Adding acids such as lemon juice, wines or vinegar to food, or alkalis such as bicarbonate of soda, may cause some destruction.

Vitamins

Some vitamins can be easily destroyed during the cooking process. This applies to the water soluble vitamins – the B-complex and C. The fat soluble vitamins – A, D, E and K – are relatively stable when heated. Some vitamin D can be lost during the grilling of fatty fish such as trout or mackerel, due to loss of oils which contain the vitamin.

Biotin is the only B-complex vitamin which is not affected by cooking. Some of the vitamins are heat stable, such as riboflavin (B2), niacin and B12, but all of them leach into the cooking liquor and losses from food of up to 30 per cent have been recorded. Some of the B-complex vitamins are destroyed by adding alkalis (such as bicarbonate of soda) to foods. For example, considerable amounts of thiamin (B1) are destroyed in bakery products when bicarbonate of soda is added.

Vitamin C is also very vulnerable to cooking as it leaches out of the food into the cooking liquor; it is very sensitive to heat and easily destroyed by the adding of alkalis. The addition of bicarbonate of soda to the water during the cooking of green vegetables so as to retain the colour of the food should be banned as it totally destroys the vitamin and thus the main nutritional benefits of eating such vegetables. A delay in serving vegetables can also cause further loss of the vitamin while the food is being kept hot. Table 5.1 shows the loss in vitamin C that occurs during the cooking of a number of different vegetables.

Table 5.1. **The effects of cooking on the vitamin C content of foods**

Vegetables	Portion	Before cooking	After cooking
Broccoli tops	100 g	110 mg	34 mg
Brussels sprouts	100 g	90 mg	40 mg
Runner beans	100 g	20 mg	5 mg
Savoy cabbage	100 g	60 mg	15 mg
Winter cabbage	100 g	55 mg	20 mg
Carrots	100 g	6 mg	4 mg
Leeks	100 g	18 mg	15 mg
Green peppers	100 g	100 mg	60 mg
Potatoes	100 g	14 mg	9 mg

How can such losses of these vitamins be minimized?
In the case of some of the B vitamins this is very difficult – for example, when thiamin is destroyed by bicarbonate of soda, and the fact that some of the vitamins will be destroyed by heat. All that can be done is to minimize the loss by ensuring that food is not subject to excessive heat, that over-cooking is avoided, and that other sources of the vitamins are provided in the diet with the help of careful menu planning. Losses of B vitamins into cooking liquor can be minimized by utilizing the liquor as part of the dish. For example, the vitamins lost when they are leached from meat during braising can be retained if the liquor is used in a sauce.

It is very important to minimize the loss of vitamin C during cooking as its food sources are limited. The following suggestions are offered:

1. Cooking the vegetables in the minimum of water. We have a habit of drowning vegetables when all that is really required is a small amount at the bottom of the pan or boiler.

2. Putting *all* vegetables in boiling water rather than putting them in cold water and then heating them. Tradition has it that root vegetables, except new potatoes, are cooked in water that starts cold, and those grown above ground are placed in boiling water. Tests have shown that vegetables cooked from cold show heavier losses of vitamin C than the same vegetables added to boiling water.

3. Utilizing liquor for stocks and soups. This is fine for home cooking but is not feasible for many catering establishments. However, it may be easier for small restaurants or pubs and inns where home-made soups are offered.

4. Pressure steaming or just steaming vegetables is a form of moist heat which will minimize the leaching of vitamin C.

5. The practice of blanching, refreshing and rechauffering vegetables when cooking to order in a hotel or restaurant is a method that does not increase the vitamin loss *as long as* the vegetables are not stored in cold water while they are waiting to be heated up.

Caterers could do a lot to minimize losses of water soluble vitamins and minerals if they cooked vegetables according to the suggestions given above and carefully planned their work to make sure the time between preparing vegetables and cooking them was as short as possible. In large-scale catering you may need to offset such losses with careful menu planning to ensure that adequate amounts of these nutrients are supplied in the diet.

Checksheet

Try to answer the following questions.

1. State the three causes of food spoilage.
    a.   b.   c.

2. Which group of vitamins deteriorate during storage?
 a. A and D   ***b.*** B and C   ***c.*** C and D   ***d.*** B and A.

3. Name three cuts of vegetables which enhance the loss of nutrients during preparation due to wastage.
 a.   ***b.***   ***c.***

4. Describe the term 'leaching'.

5. Which nutrients can be lost during cooking processes?
 a. proteins and fats
 b. fat soluble vitamins and minerals
 c. water soluble vitamins and minerals
 d. water soluble vitamins and proteins

6. Explain the process known as gelatinization.

7. List three ways in which vitamin loss in cooking can be minimized.
 a.
 b.
 c.

Now turn to the text to check your answers.

Further study

Complete the following tasks.

1. Shred 100 g of cabbage and divide it into two samples (each sample should have the same colour leaves). Cook the two samples separately in a small quantity of salted water, adding to one lot of water a pinch of bicarbonate of soda. Compare the two cooked samples for colour and texture. What effect will the bicarbonate of soda have on the vitamin content of the cabbage?

2. Collect a number of samples of perishable foods which have been invaded by moulds and/or yeasts. With the help of a magnifying glass examine and identify the number of different moulds/yeasts you can see. If you have the equipment available, look at samples of the moulds/yeasts under a microscope.

3. Can you determine why a joint of meat, when roasted in the oven, shrinks in size and if over-cooked becomes very tough? What is the effect on the meat's nutritional value?

4. What is the difference in nutritional value between a grilled pork chop and a fried pork chop?

5. Describe ways in which you can minimize the loss of vitamin C when preparing salad vegetables for a cold table.

six *What uses do convenience foods have?*

What is a **convenience food**? This is the first question which should be asked. The expression conjures up a number of responses from 'packet foods' to 'junk foods'. But the most accurate definition would be of **a food which has been processed in such a way as to extend its shelf life and reduce the preparation and cooking time**. Certainly they do not deserve the term 'junk foods'. The latter expression is a term which is frequently used to describe what are considered to be 'unhealthy' foods, and beefburgers, chips and sausages are often described as such, rather unfairly. There are, however, some very sophisticated processed foods which are merely a clever combination of chemicals. These may be very palatable, but they contain little if any natural ingredients or any which are of nutritional value. Such foods as packets of corn snacks and some desserts will be eaten in place of foods of good nutritional value. We could call them junk foods, but perhaps we should reserve this term for the choice of meals we make in our *overall* diet rather than individual foods.

If we accept the definition given above of convenience food, there are a large number of foods and food products which fall into this category. The food industry in this country has snowballed in the past 30 years, and is of prime importance in the economy both as an employer and as a major contributor to our national income. The food industry has grown to accommodate the demands from the public for a wide variety of cheap, easily prepared and cooked foods – a requirement they have succeeded in creating. We must remember that most people have limited cooking skills, little knowledge of food and minimum time to spend on the preparation and cooking of their meals. There is considerable demand today for sophisticated products which will enable people to eat a wide variety of very complex dishes without the effort of preparation and cooking. The use of microwave cookers has only fuelled this demand.

In catering the use of such products is more limited. All catering establishments will use some manufactured products in their menus, whether in the form of ingredients such as tomato paste for sauces or as actual dishes such as frozen gâteaux or pavlovas. Ten years ago extensive use was made of a wide variety of different convenience foods throughout the catering industry. Today there seems to be a swing to more 'natural' products with the use of fresh foods becoming more important – homemade soups appear on the menu instead of soups made from a packet, for example. This does not mean that convenience foods will become a thing of the past; on the contrary, the food industry is very much here to stay, but chefs appear to be more selective as to what type they use, and how often.

Methods of preservation used in preparing convenience foods

Convenience foods come in many forms but each method is designed to extend the shelf life of a product by preventing the food decaying or being contaminated by micro-organisms such as bacteria, yeast and moulds. It is beyond the scope of this book to describe in detail the various processes involved in the manufacture of different types of convenience foods. It is the nutritional implications of processing such foods which are important here. We shall therefore examine each of the main treatments with regard to the effect they have on the nutritional value of the end product.

Heat treatment

This can be by canning, sterilization, pasteurization, or ultra-heat treatment. Apart from pasteurization, all the other methods of heat treatment subject food to high temperatures which can destroy the heat-sensitive nutrients. The B-complex vitamins (particularly thiamin and folic acid) and vitamin C are most at risk, and are radically reduced during this process. Using sugar syrups for canning fruits, and brine (salt and water) for canning vegetables and meats, will cause absorption of sugar/salt into the food, thereby altering its nutritional value.

Dehydration

This method of preservation involves prolonged heat treatment (through sun drying, fluidized bed, roller drying, spray drying, or accelerated heat treatment), which destroys the heat-sensitive vitamins, especially thiamin and vitamin C. Foods with a high fat content, such as eggs and full-fat milk, can become rancid. The use of skimmed milk for drying and of hydrogenated vegetable oils have helped to overcome this problem.

Low temperature treatment

Chilling and freezing (through plate freezing, blast freezing, cryogenic freezing, cook-chill or cook-freeze) have little effect on the nutritional value of foods although there is a small loss in vitamins and minerals with prolonged storage. The greatest loss of nutrients occurs during the preparation processes before freezing, especially during the blanching of fruit and vegetables. Some of the thiamin and vitamin C content of the food is lost during this process, and some vitamins and minerals will be leached out when foods are thawed. It is important to note that in the case of freezing, foods must be in peak condition prior to processing to maintain quality. Vegetables and fruit should be harvested when their nutritional value is at its peak, and they should be frozen within hours of being picked. Thus the nutritional value of these foods will be on a par with, or often higher than, their fresh counterparts, which reach the plate via trips to markets, wholesalers, retailers, store areas and kitchens.

Before we leave this area of preservation, it is worth considering in more detail two processes which have become more widely used in catering circles: cook-chill and cook-freeze. These are forms of preservation whereby a chef will prepare a complete meal – main dish and vegetables followed by a dessert – and chill or freeze it for future use. It may be produced in individual portions or for up to a dozen or more portions. This form of catering is becoming a popular method of producing food for schools, hospitals, shift workers and hotel guests.

The cook-chill method involves food being kept chilled for a maximum of five days and then disposed of if not used, whereas cook-freeze foods will keep very much longer. With both methods, it is essential that good hygiene practices are enforced. The food is reheated for use using conventional methods or a microwave cooker. As far as the nutritional value of the end product is concerned, a lot will depend on the quality of the raw products, the method of preparation and cooking, the length of time taken for blast chilling/freezing, and the rechauffering. In all these stages nutrients are lost, especially water soluble vitamins and minerals.

Chemical treatment

The addition of salt in the form of sodium nitrate/nitrite in salting and curing, and sugar in preserves and confectionery, will alter the nutritional value of a food by increasing its mineral or carbohydrate content. Some B-complex vitamins and soluble minerals will leach out of the foods while they are soaking in brine, and heat during the curing process will also reduce the heat-sensitive B vitamins. Vitamin C will be lost in the making of preserves by exposure to high temperatures, although it can be preserved by adding acids such as vinegar. However, the addition of vinegar to foods is limited because of its flavour. Other chemical preservatives can be used with a variety of foods but are strictly controlled by the Preservatives in Food Regulations (1979). Most of these chemicals are acid-based and are specifically used for certain foods. Sulphur dioxide and sodium sulphites are widely used in preserving the prepacked, prepared vegetables (such as potatoes, carrots and cauliflowers) which are often used in catering establishments. Sulphites can destroy the vegetables' thiamin content.

Removal of air

This method of preserving foods is used for products such as bacon, cooked meats and prepared salads as well as dried goods such as coffee. If products packed in clear plastic are exposed to light, this will accelerate the loss of the light-sensitive B-complex vitamins and vitamin C.

Irradiation

Although this method of preservation and sterilization has been used since the 1950s, it has not been applied to food in this country until the 1990s. The Food Safety Act (1990) has permitted the sale of irradiated food to the public. To date it has been unpopular and it is too early to comment on the likelihood of its widespread use in the production of convenience foods. Its main use at present is to extend shelf life and to destroy micro-organisms in fresh foods. The effect on the nutrients in food varies with the type of food and the degree of radiation. Proteins and carbohydrates appear to be little changed by the process but this is not the case with fats, and high-fat foods such as milk, cheese, fatty meats and oily fish are totally unsuitable for irradiation as the structure is changed to give a very rancid flavour. Irradiation causes damage to many vitamins – vitamin A and carotene, B-complex vitamins, and vitamins C, E and K are all affected to some degree. The amount of vitamin destruction will depend on the level of radiation and the complexity of the food. Thus the vitamin C levels in fruit juice are more likely to be destroyed than those in most whole fruit. The effect of irradiation on the mineral content of foods has not been fully explored. Many nutritionists think more work should be done to obtain a complete picture of how this process affects the nutritional value of foods.

It will now be clear that nutrients undergo a number of changes in the production of convenience foods. As with the storage, preparation and cooking of fresh foods discussed in Chapter 5, we find that the water soluble vitamins – vitamin B-complex and C – and minerals are most at risk. To be fair, some food manufacturers are conscious of the nutritional loss and make efforts to minimize this, or replace the loss by **restoring** the vitamins and minerals in artificial form as in the case of white flour. Some manufacturers fortify the nutritional value of their product by adding nutrients which are not found in the natural state. The manufacturers of margarine must add vitamins A and D *by law* to their product; the manufacturers of some breakfast cereals add a number of vitamins to their products even though they are not legally obliged to do so. Other manufacturers enrich products by adding more of a nutrient than is normally present, for example extra vitamin C in fruit juices. However, the refining process inevitably leads to the loss of some nutrients. Dietary fibre is lost in the milling of wheat for white flour and the polishing of rice to produce white rice. And by removing the outer husk of grains many of the vitamins and minerals are lost.

Convenience foods are here to stay. In 1988 more than 3500 new food and drink products were launched in Britain – double the figure for 1987. An increase in public awareness of food and health will, it is hoped, encourage food manufacturers to take into account the effect of the various manufacturing processes on the nutritional value of food and to make efforts to minimize any loss. In western countries a good variety of different food and food products are included in the diet, so the losses in nutrients highlighted in this chapter can be offset. But the problems these losses can cause in countries where food is limited can result in deficiency diseases. It is important for caterers to be aware of these nutritional losses and to ensure that good menu planning will safeguard the customer.

Food additives

Public concern is at present directed not towards the nutritional losses described above but rather to the addition of a number of chemicals, known collectively as food additives, to food products. Bearing in mind that all food is really just a mixture of chemicals, some of which can be very toxic, such as the poisons in undercooked beans, it is important that we realize exactly what we mean by a food additive. Several definitions have been given of additives but perhaps the simplest is **a substance deliberately added to a food during the processing chain**. This definition covers a multitude of sins from the use of pesticides and fertilizers in the growing of food to the colours, flavours and nutrients which are added during the manufacturing process.

There are currently over 3500 different substances which are added to food during processing. They fall into four main categories:

1. **Preservatives**. These include anti-oxidants, sequestrants and chemical preservatives. There are about 63 different substances in this category.

2. **Texture modifiers**. These include emulsifiers, stabilizers and thickeners. There are about 70 substances in this group.

3. **Colour and flavour modifiers**. These include flavours, colours, flavour enhancers and sweeteners. This is the largest group and it includes over 3250 different substances.

4. **Processing aids**. These include improvers and conditioners, release agents, acids, bases, enzymes, anti-foaming agents, anti-caking agents and solvents. This group includes about 90 substances.

Some of these additives are **synthetic**, and are made in the laboratory from a wide variety of different chemicals. Others are **natural**, and are extracted from plants or animals. However, a number of complex processes using various chemicals can be involved in the extraction.

Out of the total number of food additives available for use in the food industry, only 10 per cent are controlled by a permitted list. The majority of the colours and flavours do not appear on this list. The 'E' numbers which we have become familiar with in the past few years are a way of denoting additives considered safe by the European Community. Substances on this list have undergone tests to prove their safety, and the list is constantly added to as new substances are found to be suitable, while others are removed as problems come to light or safer alternatives are found. However, the British Government also permits the use of a large number of additional substances, many of which are banned in other industrial countries. Although legislation covers the use of these additives in Britain, many nutritionists have voiced concern over the laxity in the law especially when compared with that of our European partners.

Before a substance is permitted to be added during the manufacturing process, it must pass through a number of stringent tests. These tests involve the use of animals, and result in a maximum safe quantity of the substance being decided upon. Concern has been expressed as to whether these tests really highlight the problems that food additives could cause.

In fact, in recent years there has been considerable public anxiety as to the effect a number of these additives have on our health. Certain illnesses such as dermatitis (rashes, wheels and sore and blistered skin), asthma, bronchitis and other respiratory disorders, cancer and behavioural disorders have been linked to a number of food additives. Many of these conditions occur among the food workers involved in handling the substances, but they are also found in some members of the general public. Perhaps the best publicized condition is hyperactivity in a small percentage of children. The illness causes these children to manifest extreme behaviour problems which affect their development, their progress in school as well as having a devastating effect on their family life. Hyperactivity is linked to the colouring tartrazine (E102), which is a yellow colouring added to such foods as soft drinks, confectionery and biscuits. Many manufacturers have now stopped adding this colouring to baby foods and soft drinks.

As the result of this public concern, many food manufacturers have reconsidered the necessity of adding so many food additives to products and as a result have been able to reduce the number they use. In the United States one manufacturer stopped adding artificial colours to the canned goods only to find that the canned peas were grey in colour after processing and unacceptable to the customer! Certainly, the use of food additives will continue as long as the public demands convenience foods but pressure by the public may influence their use and encourage stricter control by the Government.

Three cautionary points should be made. The first is that the tests performed on the food additives are done on the individual substance. However, in the manufacturing process a number of these substances can be added to a food – this is termed the additive cocktail – and there is no way of testing the end result of mixing these additives together. The second point can be summarized in the saying: 'We are not mice but men.' This sounds corny but it is true, and there is no guarantee that if substances are tested satisfactorily on mice they will prove harmless to humans. The only way of trying to do this would be to experiment directly on human beings – a practice that would be considered unethical. The third point is that the long-term effect of these substances on our health is not known. Unless substances are toxic, the effect of food on health is long-term and the buildup of food additives in our bodies could affect our health for decades to come.

So what advice about food additives should be given? First, that pressure by the public and the catering industry can influence the food manufacturers and the Government to tighten control of food additives.

Second, that the caterer can be selective in the manufactured products that he/she utilizes for ingredients and dishes.

How can you know which food additive is used and for what reason? By law the manufacturer must state on the product's label the ingredients that have been used, the quantity of the product, the 'best before' date, the name and address of the manufacturer and the name of the product. The manufacturer must list the food additives used in the product in the ingredients list, stating the E number or, if no number, the function and name of the substance. Some manufacturers have made a selling point by stating on the packet that the product contains 'no artificial colours or flavours'. This is no guarantee that additives have not been used but the ingredients list should show this information. By law, the manufacturer has only to state the ingredients that have been used to make the particular product, not the various food additives contained in the ingredients purchased to make the product. For example, the ingredients list on the packet of a sliced white loaf of bread will not include the 14 or so additives the miller will have put into the white flour the baker purchased to make the bread!

New regulations on the nutritional value of products have recently been passed. These instruct manufacturers to list on the label the product's total fat content, along with the maximum saturated fatty acid content. Some manufacturers have been listing the total nutritional content of their products on the labels for a few years. The common approach has been to list the protein, fat, carbohydrate, dietary fibre, calories (in mega or kilojoules as well as kilocalories), vitamin and mineral content for 100 g of the product and also for a portion size. To someone with a good knowledge of nutrition this information is very useful but it is doubtful if it causes anything other than confusion for most people. However, it is a step in the right direction although a simpler system would seem more beneficial.

Regulations also prevent manufacturers from making false claims about their product. The name of the product must reflect the ingredients, so if a product is 'beef or beef-flavoured' it must contain beef. However, if it does not contain beef but only the flavour of beef it must be called 'beef flavour'. Confusing? Perhaps a clarification in the regulations is needed. If a manufacturer produces a food which is labelled low fat or low salt or low sugar, that product must not contain more than 50 per cent of the fat, salt or sugar normally found in the product. Low-calorie foods should provide no more than 40 kcal or 167 kJ per serving or per 100 g whichever is larger. Foods claiming to be 'high in fibre' must supply a minimum of 4.2 g fibre per serving.

So where does this leave the caterer as far as convenience foods are concerned? Perhaps with the help of the information given in this chapter he/she will be a little wiser as to the nutritional losses which occur in the foods available and recognize that legislation by the Government controls some of the additions to and descriptions of food. It must also be recognized that nutritional losses occur during the preparation and cooking of fresh

food just as they do in the manufacture of convenience foods. In fact, it has been shown that some frozen vegetables and fruit contain a higher percentage of some nutrients than their fresh counterparts do. Perhaps the best advice that can be given to the caterer with regard to convenience foods versus fresh foods is that he/she should take note of the nutritional losses in each, and with careful balancing and menu planning, ensure that the losses to the customer are minimized.

Checksheet

Try to answer the following questions.

1. Define the term 'convenience foods'.

2. List six methods of food preservation.
   a.   *d.*
   b.   *e.*
   c.   *f.*

3. Which nutrients are most at risk from preservation methods?

4. Which of the following foods are unsuitable for irradiation:
   a. protein foods   *b.* fatty foods   *c.* sugary foods
   d. starchy foods.

5. Define the term 'food additive'.

6. State the four major functions of food additives.
   a.   *c.*
   b.   *d.*

7. Explain the difference between a 'synthetic' and a 'natural' additive.

8. What percentage of food additives are controlled by a permitted list?
_____ per cent.

9. Describe what is meant by an E number.

10. State two illnesses which have been linked with food additives.
   a.   *b.*

Now turn to the text to check your answers.

Further study

Complete the following tasks.

1. Collect labels off ten manufactured foods. With the help of a book or leaflet on E numbers (see suggestions in 'Useful Books for Further Reading'), identify the food additives given on the labels and determine the function of each in the product.

2. Keep a diary of your food intake for five days. Identify and list the 'convenience foods' you eat. What proportion of your diet is made up of such foods?

seven

Food and health

Having studied how the body uses food, what the components of food are, and how they can be affected by different processes, we shall now turn our attention to how we can ensure that our bodies receive the correct balance of the various nutrients. This chapter will explore the concept of a balanced diet and endeavour to find a way of checking if the balance is correct for ourselves and for our customers. We shall also look at how much our bodies need of the various nutrients and the effects an imbalance in nutrients has on our health.

What is a balanced diet?

There have been many definitions given to describe what a balanced diet is made up of, the most common being 'the correct amount of each nutrient to ensure good health'. This sounds very good, but it is also very vague, giving no idea as to how this can be achieved. Probably the clearest recent definition appeared in the ILEA *Nutritional Guidelines*:

A balanced diet is one which provides:
– an adequate amount of food energy
– optimum proportions of protein, starch and fat
– sufficient dietary fibre
– an adequate amount of minerals, trace metals, vitamins and essential fatty acids.

If a diet meets an individual's energy needs and comprises a mixture of cereal foods (e.g. bread, pasta, rice, breakfast cereals, biscuits), vegetables and fruits with some milk, milk products, meat, fish, eggs or pulses, and small quantities of fats and oils, then adequate amounts of nutrients should be present.

According to this definition, a good diet should be based on cereal foods, vegetables and fruit with other foods adding the 'frills' to our meals, to ensure a good balance of nutrients. This is significantly different to the normal British diet, which is based on a higher percentage of animal products than plant products. It does not necessarily advocate a vegetarian diet but merely emphasizes the foods which will supply the necessary nutrients. It also emphasizes the need to eat a good variety of foods in our daily diet so that our bodies get the nutrients they require. However, it is also important that the variety comes in the right mixture.

How do we know if our diet is balanced?

Before we look at ways in which we can check if a diet is balanced or not we need to decide how many nutrients we really need to keep our bodies fit. For some years the Government in the shape of the Department of Health and Social Security (DHSS, now the Department of Health) have provided guidelines in the form of **recommended daily amounts** of nutrients (RDAs) to indicate the nutritional needs of groups of people in Britain. A major revision of the RDAs has been performed by COMA (Committee on Medical Aspects) and this was published in 1991. The revision is a culmination of the work pioneered by NACNE and COMA in the early 1980s, which will be discussed later in the chapter. The new guidelines have been renamed **dietary reference values** (DRVs) and provide comprehensive tables for each of the major nutrients – proteins, fats, sugars and starches, non-starch polysaccharides (dietary fibre), 13 vitamins and 11 minerals – as well as energy. COMA has given the **estimated average requirement** (EAR) for energy and for each nutrient; this tells us the average quantity that will cater for most individuals' needs. However, COMA also gives a range for each nutrient in the shape of **lower reference nutrient intake** (LRNI) and **reference nutrient intake** (RNI) to indicate minimum and maximum figures.

An example of the DRVs is given in Table 7.1 with the EARs for energy, protein and iron. It can be seen that the population is divided into age and sex groups, but no account is taken of height or build or that (to take the two extremes of one age span) 19-year-olds are probably physically more active in their social life than 50-year-olds! To be fair to the DRVs it is a daunting task to try to cater for all the population's nutritional needs and lifestyles at the same time and thus it is important to emphasize that these figures are intended as guidelines only.

Food tables

But how can we interpret these guidelines in terms of food, meals and a balanced diet? Food tables list the nutrient content of many basic commodities as well as of processed foods. These tables, available in book form and now also on computer software, have been devised by food scientists and nutritionists after painstaking laboratory work to identify the quantity of nutrients present in individual foods. Many food manufacturers supply such information on the packaging of their products.

With the use of these food tables, it is possible to build up a balanced daily diet for an individual or even a group of people, such as children in school or the elderly in residential homes. This can be achieved by calculating the quantity of food needed to supply the correct amount of nutrients. Alternatively, it is possible to determine if a person's diet is balanced or not by weighing the foods that an individual consumes, and calculating, with the help of the food tables, how many nutrients they have received. However, this is an extremely time-consuming task and one that can only

Table 7.1. **Dietary reference values for food energy and nutrients for the United Kingdom, 1991: estimated average requirements (EAR) for food energy, protein and iron**

Age	Energy kcals/d (MJ/d)		Protein g/d		Iron mg/d	
	Males	Females				
0–3 mths	545 (2.28)	515 (2.16)	—		1.3	
4–6 mths	690 (2.89)	645 (2.69)	10.6		3.3	
7–9 mths	825 (3.44)	765 (3.20)	11.0		6.0	
10–12 mths	920 (3.85)	865 (3.61)	11.2		6.0	
1–3 yrs	1230 (5.15)	1165 (4.86)	11.7		5.3	
4–6 yrs	1715 (7.16)	1545 (6.46)	14.8		4.7	
7–10 yrs	1970 (8.24)	1740 (7.28)	22.8		6.7	
			Males	Females	Males	Females
11–14 yrs	2220 (9.27)	1845 (7.92)	33.8	33.1	8.7	11.4*
15–18 yrs	2755 (11.51)	2110 (8.83)	46.1	37.1	8.7	11.4*
19–50 yrs	2550 (10.60)	1940 (8.10)	44.4	36.0	6.7	11.4*
51–59 yrs	2550 (10.60)	1900 (8.00)	42.6	37.2	6.7	6.7
60–64 yrs	2380 (9.93)	1900 (7.99)	42.6	37.2	6.7	6.7
65–74 yrs	2330 (9.71)	1900 (7.96)	42.6	37.2	6.7	6.7
75 + yrs	2100 (8.77)	1810 (7.61)	42.6	37.2	6.7	6.7

*About 10% of women with very high menstrual losses will require more iron than shown.

More detailed tables for all the nutrients will be found in *Dietary Reference Values for Food, Energy and Nutrients for the United Kingdom*, Report on Health and Social Subjects 41, HMSO 1991.

be achieved if you have an unlimited amount of time and incredible patience, even with the help of a calculator or a computer. It would involve calculating the nutrient content of the foods to be included in a meal and checking and adjusting to ensure that the correct amount of nutrients were present. It is obvious that this is beyond the scope of most people and certainly chefs and catering managers have little time in a day to accomplish this task, which tends to be left to experts such as dietitians and nutritionists. So there must be a more practical and easier method of checking if a diet is balanced or not.

Food groups

One of the most useful ways of producing and checking a balanced diet is to separate foods into groups. Various groupings have been suggested over the years, based on nutrients, functions of nutrients, or even single foods. But the most practical grouping, produced by the Health Departments of

Great Britain and Northern Ireland in 1978, is based on dividing foods into eight main commodity groups as follows:

1. Breads and cereals
2. Meat, fish and eggs
3. Milk and dairy food
4. Fruit and vegetables
5. Non-dairy fats
6. Preserves
7. Confectionery
8. Alcohol

This method incorporates as many foods as possible into workable groups. Table 7.2 lists the food groups giving examples of foods within each group and the major nutrients represented by those groups.

This method of grouping is sensible and simplistic but still poses a few problems. Some foods do not fit neatly into groups: for example should cakes and biscuits be in the bread and cereal group rather than in confectionery? Do eggs really fit into the meat and fish group? Should pulses be in the meat, fish and egg group as an alternative form of protein? Any method is open to criticism and it is not easy to divide so many differing foods into a group system but this method seems workable if at times limiting.

How can these food groups be used to help balance a diet? First look carefully again at Table 7.2. It will become clear that the first four groups mentioned (breads and cereals; meat, fish and eggs; milk and dairy food; fruit and vegetables) provide a wide variety of nutrients between them. Compare them with the remaining groups (non-dairy fats; preserves; confectionery; and alcohol), the nutrient content of which is very limited. **If the diet consists of foods mainly from the first four food groups it will supply a wide variety of nutrients and is more likely to be nutritionally balanced.** If on the other hand the second four groups are more widely represented in the diet, the supply of nutrients will be more limited, making the diet nutritionally inadequate. The first four groups are thus known as the **primary food groups** (see Figure 7.1).

The 'food group method' as a means of judging whether a meal or a daily diet is balanced or not is a beautifully simple idea which is quick and easy to implement. However, a word of caution is important. This method can only provide a *guide* to a balanced diet, not an accurate calculation, which can only be achieved by using food tables. It is very difficult to produce accurate dietary information for an individual or groups of people as there are so many variables to be taken into consideration. Nevertheless, this is still a useful method for chefs and catering managers to use when planning

Milk and milk products
(cheese, yogurt)

Cereal foods (bread,
breakfast cereals, etc.)

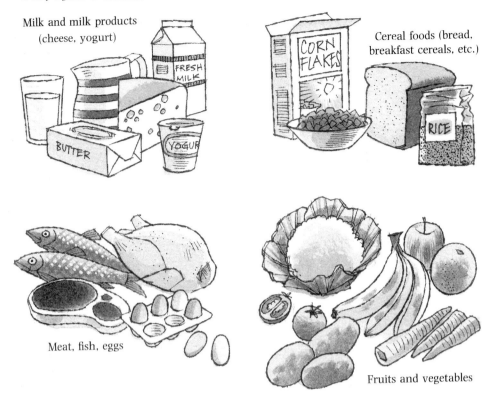

Meat, fish, eggs

Fruits and vegetables

Figure 7.1   The primary food groups

menus. Turn to Appendix II for a comprehensive guide to how to use this method to check the nutritional balance of a menu.

Why is it so important to have a balanced diet?

It is necessary to include all the nutrients in our diet in a reasonable proportion to ensure good health is maintained. Our bodies can only function correctly and perform the tasks we require them to do if they are supplied with the right quantities of nutrients from our diet. Sadly there is no trigger mechanism in our brains to tell us which nutrients we are short of or which ones we should not be including as there is already a glut in our bodies. If we possessed such a mechanism, our health would be greatly improved. We can easily convince ourselves we are hungry, or crave sweet foods and believe that our bodies really need them. But it is literally 'all in our minds'. Our choices of food will obviously greatly influence whether we get a good balance or not, and unfortunately these are subject to many influences which have nothing to do with our nutritional needs.

Table 7.2. **The principal food groups in the British diet**

Group	Typical foods	Major nutrients
1. Bread and cereals	Bread Cereals, e.g. rice Porridge Breakfast cereals Pasta Flour	Carbohydrate Protein Dietary fibre Vitamins – B group Minerals
2. Meat, fish and eggs	Meat Fish Offal Poultry Eggs	Protein Fat Vitamins – A, D, B group Minerals – iron
3. Milk and dairy food	Milk Cheese Yogurt Cream Butter	Protein Carbohydrate Fat Vitamins – A and D Minerals – calcium
4. Fruit and vegetables	All fruits Fruit juice Potatoes Leaf vegetables Salad vegetables Root vegetables Pulses (peas, beans, lentils)	Protein (from pulses) Carbohydrate Dietary fibre Vitamins – C, carotene Minerals
5. Non-dairy fats	Suet Dripping Lard Vegetable oils	Fat Vitamins – A and D
6. Preserves	Sugar Honey Jam Marmalade Syrup Treacle	Carbohydrate
7. Confectionery	Soft drinks Sweets Chocolate Cakes Biscuits	Carbohydrate Fat
8. Alcohol	Wines Sherries Beers Spirits Liquors	Carbohydrate Alcohol

Recent studies have shown that children are greatly influenced by television advertisements for foods and soft drinks. Although individually these foods cannot be termed 'junk foods', together they contribute to a 'junk diet' full of snacks, sugary and fatty foods, which take the place of foods which would supply valuable nutrients.

Diseases of undernutrition

That there is an important relationship between our diet and our health has been clear for some time. If we do not have sufficient of one or more nutrients we develop what are termed **deficiency diseases**. Some of these have been well documented for centuries. Unfortunately, in many parts of the world whole populations suffer greatly from such deficiencies, due to an inadequate diet which is either lacking in variety or which simply does not contain enough food. These deficiency diseases are caused by **undernutrition**, and can be categorized as follows:

Lack of protein causes a condition known as kwashokor, with symptoms of muscle wastage, loss of hair, ulceration and water retention, resulting in a pot belly.

Lack of carbohydrate and fat can cause severe loss of weight, lack of energy, lethargy and an inability to maintain body temperature and fight infection.

Lack of dietary fibre can result in constipation, diverticulitis and cancer of the bowel.

Lack of vitamin A (retinol) causes 'night blindness' resulting in permanent blindness and failure of the lubricating system of the body which causes the skin and the various tubes of the body (e.g. the oesophagus, nasal and respiratory tubes) to dry up.

Lack of vitamin B1 (thiamin) results in a nervous disorder known as beri-beri.

Lack of vitamin B2 (riboflavin) stunts the growth of children and causes a sore tongue, a form of skin irritation and painful fissures around the mouth, in adults.

Lack of niacin (nicotinic acid) causes a condition known as pellagra with symptoms of sore tongue, diarrhoea, lesions of the skin, mental confusion and depression.

Lack of vitamin B6 (pyridoxin) can cause various symptoms ranging from soreness of the mouth, a form of eczema, irritability, depression and nausea. It has been known to cause convulsions in babies.

Lack of vitamin B12 results in a condition known as pernicious anaemia, where the bone marrow produces fewer red blood cells which are immature. In addition, mental disturbance may also occur.

Lack of vitamin C (ascorbic acid) results in a condition known as scurvy with symptoms of tiredness, depression, and haemorrhaging (causing bruising especially around the joints, swollen gums and loosened teeth, and internal bleeding which will result in death).

Lack of vitamin D (calciferol) causes bone conditions known as rickets in children and osteomalacia in adults.

Lack of the mineral iron causes anaemia with the symptoms of tiredness, weakness and lack of energy.

Lack of calcium causes rickets in children and osteomalacia in adults.

Lack of the trace elements in the diet, such as copper, selenium and zinc, can result in poor health and inability to thrive in children. At the moment, studies are being undertaken to determine more specific effects.

Lack of water brings about rapid dehydration and an inability of the body to function.

These deficiency diseases are rare in the more affluent western world and many are virtually unheard of in Britain. Lack of iron and calcium can occur in some groups but deficiencies are not prevalent. The only deficiency that is common in Britain (though it is less of a problem in the Third World) is dietary fibre. In the past ten years research has shown that lack of dietary fibre, caused especially by our consumption of refined cereals, has resulted in a number of digestive tract diseases such as constipation, diverticulitis and cancer of the bowel.

Diseases of overnutrition

In Britain and other industrial countries we eat a more varied diet than people in other parts of the world: we eat both animal and plant foods and our meals change from day to day in their content. Consequently our ability to eat a balanced diet is enhanced. This is more by luck than judgement as generally our knowledge of the potential nutrients available to us in the food we eat is very limited. Not only do we eat a varied diet but we have a vast array of foods to choose from. So it may come as something of a surprise to realize that not only do the majority of the population not have a balanced diet but they also suffer from **malnutrition** in the form of **overnutrition**. This is where an excess of one or more nutrients is consumed, which bring about a number of conditions resulting in ill health.

It may seem strange, but it is only in the past 10–15 years that the problem of overnutrition in Britain has been studied and recognized for what it is. The large variety of foods and food products that have been available to us since the 1960s has resulted in an increase in the number of conditions affecting our health which have a direct link with an excess of nutrients. The types of conditions and their link with excess nutrients and foods are listed below:

Dental caries (tooth decay), linked with eating a diet high in sugar and sugary foods giving an excess of carbohydrates.

Overweight, linked with a diet high in sugar, sugary foods, fats and fatty foods resulting in an excess of carbohydrate and fat.

Diabetes, particularly the non-insulin dependent diabetes (see Chapter 9 for details) could have a link with the amount of sugar and sugary foods included in the diet over a long period of time.

Heart disease, including heart attacks, strokes, thrombosis, angina, atherosclerosis and high blood pressure, is linked to high levels of fats, especially animal fats, in the diet.

High blood pressure (hypertension) can result from excess amounts of salt (sodium chloride) in the diet over a long period of time.

There are three major factors worth emphasizing. The first is that diet is not the sole cause of these conditions, although it is a very important factor. Lack of exercise, smoking, excessive stress levels and genetic factors can also play a part. Second, these illnesses are a result of the long-term effect of excess nutrients over a period of time stretching to decades, not just a few months or a few years. Third, these illnesses are no respecter of persons. I have often heard the comment: 'I'm all right, I don't have a weight problem, I burn up all my fat so I don't need to worry about what I eat.' Unfortunately for them, this is not true. Thin, fat, tall, short, small-boned or big-boned – all people are what they eat and these illnesses can affect us all.

The NACNE and COMA reports

The relationship between diet and health was highlighted in 1983 with the publication of the discussion paper *Proposals for Nutritional Guidelines for Health Education in Britain,* by the National Advisory Committee on Nutrition Education (popularly known as **NACNE**). This paper was the culmination of discussions and studies by concerned experts into the relationship between diet and health. The NACNE report was closely followed in 1984 by another called *Diet and Cardiovascular Disease* produced by the Committee on Medical Aspects of Food Policy, known as **COMA**. The COMA report dealt primarily with heart disease but the recommendations made followed very closely those set out in the NACNE report.

The conclusions reached and the recommendations given by both reports have been widely publicized over the years and have influenced many people to alter their diet to comply with the advice given. These reports recommended that we should **lower the quantity of sugar, fat and salt** we have in our diet and **increase the amount of dietary fibre**, especially from cereal sources.

The reports also recommended a change in emphasis in our diet to ensure a more balanced approach to nutrients, in order to ensure a decrease in the number of diet-related illnesses. Rather than concentrate on nutrients, the two committees looked at studies showing the average total daily energy intake levels of the adult population and the percentage of energy obtained from protein, fats and carbohydrates. They found that for most adults, the energy supplied from foods was as follows:

> 12 per cent of energy was obtained from proteins.
>
> 43 per cent of energy was obtained from fats.
>
> 45 per cent of energy was obtained from carbohydrates.

The committee concluded that these proportions needed changing to the following:

> 12 per cent of energy from proteins.
>
> 35 per cent of energy from fats.
>
> 53 per cent of energy from carbohydrates.

To achieve these changes and ensure a balanced diet, the recommendations suggest cutting down the fat in the diet from both animal and vegetable sources. To ensure energy levels are maintained it is important to increase the amount of carbohydrate in the diet, not from sugar and sugary foods but from cereal-based products, particularly the unrefined cereals. By following these guidelines, excesses of some of the nutrients are reduced but adequate supplies of protein, vitamins and minerals are maintained. The reports concluded that our high intake of salt and alcohol should also be reduced.

These, then, are the nutritional guidelines which should provide us with a balanced diet to maintain good health. They have been popularized over the past few years by the term 'healthy eating'. This is an unfortunate term for what is a sensible approach to our diet, conjuring up as it does something different to normal, something special, whereas it is in fact a slight readjustment of our normal eating pattern.

This concept of a balanced diet has many implications for the foods we eat and the way we cook them. The significance for chefs and caterers is considerable. The next chapter will attempt to explain the reasons behind the guidelines in more detail and will examine the practical implications for catering.

Checksheet

Try to answer the following questions.

1. What do the initials DRV stand for?

2. How many kilocalories will a 17-year-old girl require each day?
   a. 1000 kcals   *b.* 1150 kcals   *c.* 2000 kcals   *d.* 2150 kcals

3. How much vitamin C should an adult man have each day?
   a. 20 mg   *b.* 25 mg   *c.* 30 mg   *d.* 60 mg

4. List the eight food groups.
   a.   *e.*
   b.   *f.*
   c.   *g.*
   d.   *h.*

5. Name the four primary food groups.
   a.
   b.
   c.
   d.

6. Why are these groups termed primary food groups?

7. Complete the following:
   a. Lack of protein causes
   b. Lack of vitamin A causes
   c. Lack of vitamin C causes
   d. Lack of iron causes
   e. Too much sugar can cause
   f. Too much fat and sugar can cause
   g. Too much salt can cause
   h. Too much animal fat can cause

8. What does NACNE stand for?

9. Nutritional guidelines encourage us to lower the _____, _____, and _____ content of our diet and increase _____ _____ intake especially from _____ foods.

10. What is the recommended percentage of daily energy from different nutrients?
   _____% from proteins
   _____% from fats
   _____% from carbohydrates

Now turn to the text to check your answers.

Further study

Complete the following tasks.

1. Keep a diary of your food intake for two days, making a record of the weights of the food you have eaten. With the help of food tables, work out how much protein, energy (kilocalories/kilojoules) and iron you have had each day. How does the result compare with the DRV for your age.

2. Using the food diary from Task 1 determine if you have had a balanced diet with the help of the food group method. Appendix II explains the process.

3. Compare the procedure of calculating food intakes by food tables with that of the food group method.

4. List ways in which a caterer could reduce the fat, sugar and salt content of a menu and increase dietary fibre. Compare your answers with the suggestions in Chapter 8.

Recipe for health

In this section we will endeavour to 'put the meat on the bones' of the concept of sensible eating, a preferable term to healthy eating, which was introduced in the final part of Chapter 7. To recap, the nutritional guidelines recommended by NACNE and COMA suggest that we should lower our intake of sugar, fat and salt and add more fibre foods to our diet. So what does this really mean?

Sugar versus our teeth, our weight and our health

For some time it has been known that sugar has a direct effect on our teeth, and excessive amounts cause **tooth decay** or **dental caries**. The bacteria naturally present in our mouths feed on the sugar in our diet. The waste products produced by these bacteria are acidic and attack the enamel on our teeth, hastening tooth decay. The Health Education Council (now the Health Education Authority), in conjunction with the dental profession, started a campaign in schools some years ago to try to encourage children to reduce the amount of sugar, sweets and chocolates in their diet. This campaign was very successful and there was a noticeable reduction in tooth decay among children at that time.

It is estimated that over half the adult population of Britain is following some form of weight reduction regime at any one time! Weight problems are not the prerogative of affluent countries alone and it is a gross over-simplification to state that people are fat because they overeat. In many cases, thin people eat far more food than fat people, and there are factors about weight and why some people gain it easily that have baffled experts for some time. Lack of physical exercise, sedentary work and genetic factors play a part, and a diet full of concentrated energy foods will cause some people to gain weight rapidly. Being **overweight** brings its own health problems, such as back strain, hiatus hernia, varicose veins, as well as a greater risk of diabetes, high blood pressure and heart disease, not to mention the social pressure to be slim, and poor self-image.

Sugar and sugar-rich foods form a concentrated source of energy – in fact sugar is referred to in nutrition circles as 'empty' calories as it is one of very few foods which only contain one nutrient, supplying only energy in the diet. A diet high in sugar and sugary foods is likely to lead to weight problems. However, we must not forget that fat also supplies a high proportion of energy to the body. So a combination of high-sugar and high-fat intake in a diet is a recipe for disaster for those people who gain weight easily.

A long-term diet which is high in sugar and sugar-rich foods is thought to be a contributing factor in the development of **diabetes** in the middle-aged and the elderly. Diabetes is a condition brought on by the body's inability to produce enough, if any, of a hormone called insulin. Insulin regulates the amount of glucose present in the blood at any one time. In Chapter 3, we discussed how carbohydrates – sugars and starches – are used by the body in the form of glucose to produce energy, and that glucose, which itself is a simple sugar, is transported to every cell of the body via the bloodstream. So at certain times of the day – several hours after eating a meal containing foods rich in sugar or starch – the level of glucose in the blood will rise due to an influx from the digestive tract. Too much glucose in the blood would have a disastrous effect as it would turn the blood into a syrup which would impede the flow. To counteract this effect, the body produces the hormone insulin, which converts any excess glucose into an insoluble substance which is then stored in the liver or in muscle cells.

If insulin is either not produced at all or in insufficient quantities, there is a buildup of glucose in the blood and this brings about the condition known as diabetes. To overcome this problem the body takes emergency action by trying to get rid of the glucose by other means. It achieves this by allowing the sugar to be released into the urine via the kidneys, something that does not usually happen. To do this more fluid must be taken into the body and one of the symptoms of diabetes is extreme thirst. Another symptom is infection in the urinary tract as the sugar in the urine acts as an irritant. Too much glucose in the blood can also affect the eyesight. If untreated the person's health will gradually deteriorate and death could occur.

There are two main forms of diabetes. The first is Type 1 or insulin-dependent diabetes, where the body produces no insulin. This type affects young children and young adults and is thought to be genetically linked or could be caused by a virus. It is treated by daily injections of insulin and by a special diet. The other form of diabetes is known as Type 2 or non-insulin-dependent, where the body is producing some insulin but not sufficient to cope. It is this latter type which is considered to have a link with a diet which is too rich, over a long period, in carbohydrates, particularly sugar. It is becoming more common among the middle-aged and the elderly, and is treated by following a special diet and sometimes by also taking tablets which encourage the body to produce more insulin. Dietary treatment of this condition will be discussed in Chapter 9 along with weight reduction diets.

Reducing our sugar intake

As we have discovered, carbohydrates consist of sugars, starches and dietary fibre. We are here most interested in sugars, sucrose in particular. Each person in Britain consumes up to 40 kg of sucrose each year, mainly in the form of the white packet sugar we use as a sweetener in numerous foods. If we could reduce this figure by over half we would have 'cracked it' – so to speak! How can this be done? It is not always easy as a 'sweet' taste becomes a habit we have developed, often from birth, and it is a habit which has to be broken. Here are some simple guidelines:

1. Add less sugar to drinks such as tea or coffee or better still cut it out completely.

2. Eat fewer sweets, chocolates, snack bars, jams, honey and preserves.

3. Find alternatives to fruit canned in syrup, sugar-coated breakfast cereals, fizzy drinks and squashes.

4. Eat fewer iced cakes and biscuits, and desserts which contain high proportions of sugar.

This is how an individual can reduce their own intake but how do the guidelines relate to the caterer? The same general principles apply but by studying the menu on offer to the customer it is possible to supply some low-sugar alternatives.

---

1. Offer artificial sweeteners for customers' use with tea and coffee.

2. Include unsweetened fruit juices and breakfast cereals or dried fruit compote for the breakfast menu, along with a fruit purée conserve, as an alternative to marmalades and preserves.

3. Offer low-calorie fizzy drinks and mixer drinks in the bar along with a cellar of good dry wines and fortified wines!

4. Include several desserts on lunch or dinner menus that have a

---

low sugar content. Fresh fruit salad is the classic example – but made without the sugar syrup! If necessary, study the recipes of various desserts and decide if it is possible to reduce the sugar content or use an alternative source of sweetener, such as the natural sugars present in dried fruits. This is where the chef's culinary skills and creative talents come to the fore.

5. Experiment with recipes for cakes or gâteaux by adding less sugar. Do we really have to follow a recipe exactly? Will the end product be any different in appearance or texture if the sugar content is reduced? Try and see. Alternatively, research recipes containing less sugar, to produce as an optional choice on a sweet trolley.

6. Take care when you use convenience foods. When sugar appears near the top of the ingredients list it is guaranteed to be a major constituent of the food. Manufacturers are now producing low-sugar alternatives, like fruit canned in natural juices.

It is hoped that these guidelines will be of use to the chef and will act as a springboard for other ideas.

Fats and heart disease

There has been a gradual increase over the years in the incidence of heart disease in this country. Britain is one of the world leaders in the number of deaths each year from this disease and Scotland boasts the highest number of fatalities. It is a condition common in the affluent West but not in underdeveloped countries. Evidence of the link between diet and heart disease has been growing over the years, although it must be emphasized that diet is not the only factor, even if it is a major contributor.

The relationship between fats and heart disease is an interesting one. A high intake of fats, particularly the animal fats which contain a high proportion of saturated fatty acids, encourages the liver to over-produce a substance called **cholesterol**. Produced naturally by the liver, it is a very important substance required by all cells of the body. It is involved in the structure of the cell and is of vital importance to us even though it has received a 'bad press' for the past few years. The liver forms cholesterol from a number of raw materials including fatty substances and it is transported to all parts of the body by the blood.

If too much cholesterol is produced, it starts to build up in the bends of the arteries and veins as it travels around the body. (This is a similar process to the silting up of a river bed as the river meanders through the final part of its journey to the sea.) The result of this buildup is a reduction in size of the diameter of the arteries and veins, as illustrated in Figure 8.1. When

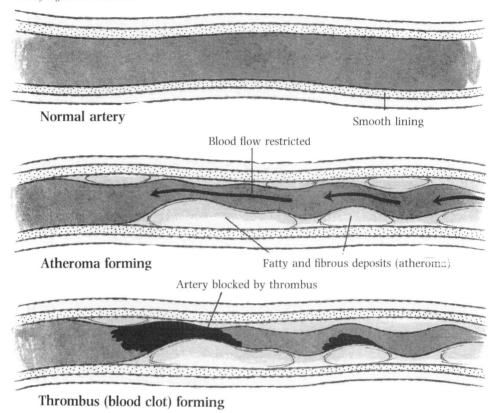

Normal artery

Smooth lining

Blood flow restricted

Atheroma forming

Fatty and fibrous deposits (atheroma)

Artery blocked by thrombus

Thrombus (blood clot) forming

Figure 8.1   The effect of a cholesterol buildup in the veins and arteries

this occurs, it is known as **atherosclerosis** or hardening of the arteries. Because the diameter of the arteries and veins is reduced in size, the same amount of blood has to be forced through a smaller space. This causes the pressure to rise, resulting in high blood pressure or hypertension. This in turn causes the heart to pump harder and so creates more strain for the heart muscles; angina can develop, the heart can go into spasm, and a heart attack can result.

Another problem with the buildup of cholesterol is that a blood clot can develop which could block the artery or vein completely. We all produce blood clots from time to time – they are formed from debris from dead cells and other waste materials. As long as the blood system remains unobstructed, these clots will cause no harm and will be dispersed by natural processes. But if there is an obstruction in the system, like a buildup of cholesterol, the blood clot would not be able to pass through, and this would cause a total blockage known as a **thrombosis**. This will stop the flow of blood, which means the cells no longer have access to oxygen. When this happens in the artery leading to the brain, resulting in the brain becoming starved of oxygen, a stroke occurs. If the blood flow stops, the heart will not pump and a heart attack occurs. A heart attack is often fatal and even if the individual survives, there is permanent damage done to the heart.

The saturated fats are those fats which contain a high percentage of saturated fatty acids. The majority of these come from animal sources such as butter, lard, suet, hard margarines, fatty meats, cheese, whole-milk

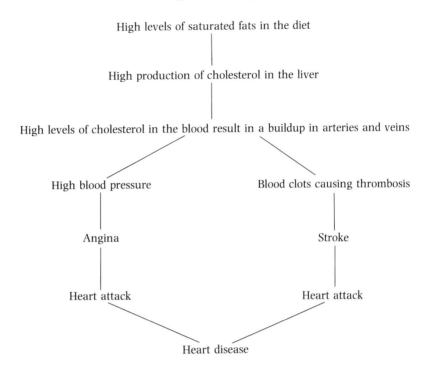

High levels of saturated fats in the diet

High production of cholesterol in the liver

High levels of cholesterol in the blood result in a buildup in arteries and veins

High blood pressure

Blood clots causing thrombosis

Angina

Stroke

Heart attack

Heart attack

Heart disease

Figure 8.2 Summary of the relationship between fats and heart disease

cream, and foods containing animal fat such as pastry, cakes and biscuits. A diet containing the mono- and polyunsaturated fats, that is those from vegetable sources – the vegetable oils, the soft margarines, nuts and oily fish – does not encourage the over-production of cholesterol by the liver but it does not significantly reduce it either. The advice from the NACNE and COMA reports is to reduce the total fat content of the diet by half, especially the animal (saturated) fats, but also the vegetable (mono- and polyunsaturated) fats as well. Recent studies, however, show that if we include oily fish (like sardines, herring and mackerel), which contain essential fatty acids, in our diet, then this is beneficial to health and can help prevent heart disease.

Reducing our fat intake

The following guidelines will help to reduce the fat content in our diet:

1. Spread butter or margarine sparingly. It is preferable to use a margarine which claims on the label to be 'high in polyunsaturates'. (This is not strictly true but it will contain more polyunsaturated fatty acids than other types of margarine.) Alternatively use low-fat spreads.

2. Avoid fried foods, and try other methods of cooking such as grilling, baking, poaching and boiling. When roasting or braising use vegetable oils sparingly.

3. Cut the visible fat off meat and eat more of the leaner types of meat such as chicken, turkey, venison, rabbit and offal. Include white fish, which is low in fat, but also have a serving of oily fish two to three times a week.

4. Avoid eating too many pastries, puddings, pies, rich cakes and biscuits.

5. Watch your intake of dairy foods, especially whole milk, cream and high-fat cheeses. Table 8.1 lists the percentage fat content of a number of different cheeses – it can be seen that cheese can be considered a high-fat food. Try some low-fat alternatives such as semi-skimmed or skimmed milk, low-fat yogurt, fromage frais and quark and also some low-fat cheeses.

6. Remember that many snack foods, such as crisps, chocolate and snack bars, have a high fat content.

How can the caterer translate these guidelines into good practices for his/her establishment? Here are some suggestions which I hope will stimulate further ideas for helping to cut the fat intake of customers' meals by half.

---

1. Offer a selection of low-fat spreads and soft margarines.

2. Include as many different methods of cooking as possible and cut down on fried foods. Care should be taken when coating foods for grilling with fat. Only use oil very sparingly and where possible avoid completely.

3. Use only vegetable oils which contain polyunsaturated fatty acids like sunflower oil, corn oil, soya bean oil or rapeseed oil, rather than cheaper blended vegetable oils. Olive oil, a monounsaturated oil, is good but expensive. Avoid solid vegetable fats as these contain saturated fats.

4. Include different types of meat on the menu, especially those low in fat. Beef, lamb and pork are all fairly high in fat, even containing fat in the lean muscle. Varying the meats and using lean cuts, including the less-expensive poultry and offal, will reduce the fat content.

5. Include both white and oily fish on the menu – grilling and poaching will keep the fat content of the meal down.

6. Add some bean dishes as well as using low-fat milk and cheeses for the vegetarian choice.

7. Ensure that there are alternatives to chips on a menu and avoid glazing vegetables with fat and adding roux-based sauces.

8. Use skimmed milk powder in cooking: it is cheaper than whole-

---

milk powder and keeps better. Use semi-skimmed or skimmed milk for drinks and introduce low-fat cheese on the cheese board. Table 8.1 lists the fat content of a number of cheeses.

9. Check how often pastries appear on the menu. If they appear too often, cut back on their use.

10. Try alternatives to cream, such as fromage frais or quark. Use natural yogurt, which is more economical than cream but gives an acidic flavour. Using single or half-fat cream is better than double cream.

Table 8.1. **The fat content of various cheeses**

Types of cheese	Fat content (%)	Types of cheese	Fat content (%)
Cream cheese	50	Processed cheese	25
Stilton	40	Brie	22
Cheddar	30	Camembert	22
Cheshire	30	Edam	22
Double Gloucester	30	Low-fat cheese	15
		Cottage cheese	4

Salt and high blood pressure

Salt consists of two elements – sodium and chlorine – and both are required to maintain and balance the fluid levels of the body. The link between salt and our health is that by including high levels of salt in our diet over a long period of time, there is a risk that we may develop high blood pressure. This in turn could lead to a stroke or heart disease.

Salt has been a vital part of our lives for centuries. The Romans were paid in salt instead of money and numerous wars have been fought over salt mines. For our ancestors, it was a very important commodity as 'salting food' was the only way to preserve it over the non-growing season (i.e. late autumn, winter, early spring), and meant the choice between life or starvation.

However, it is only in this century that we have increased our intake of salt (sodium chloride). The body requires between 5 g and 9 g each day. That is about one or two level teaspoons. Most of us would consider that we eat far less than that, whereas in fact studies show the average intake to be 15 g to 20 g (three to four teaspoons) a day and many people are in excess of this figure.

The body has an excellent mechanism for controlling the quantity of sodium in our bodies. If there is too much, the kidneys will filter it out and expel it in the urine. If there is too little, the kidneys will conserve it. Some sodium is lost in sweat but this only becomes a problem for people living in tropical climates or who are international sportsmen or sportswomen. So, if the body can cope well with the amount of salt we take in our diet, why is it a problem?

The problem appears to be that if we keep this mechanism working overtime because we consume three or four times more salt than our body needs every day, then there comes a time when the system starts to break down due to overwork. Like any machine that works non-stop for some time, it starts to wear down and parts go wrong. So after decades of coping with too much salt in the diet, the body system starts to wear down, the kidneys cannot cope so well and high blood pressure results.

There are only four foods which naturally contain sodium. These are **meat, fish, milk** and **eggs**. Vegetables, fruit, nuts and cereals do not naturally contain sodium, but the majority of our manufactured foods have salt added to them. We not only use salt as a preservative but it is also widely used as a flavouring, so the majority of the foods we eat now contain salt. Table 8.2 lists a varied selection of foods along with their salt content. Most of the salt is added during preparation, cooking or manufacture. As you can see, the total salt content for all the foods shown is 5 g, which equals the amount of salt our body needs in one day. Perhaps now it can be seen why our intake is so high, as most of us eat much more than just these foods in one day!

Table 8.2. **The salt content of a number of foods**

Food	Quantity	Salt content
Sausages	2	2.5 g
Ham	1 slice	1.0 g
Bread	2 slices	0.8 g
Cheese	25 g	0.4 g
Unsalted crisps	1 packet	0.3 g
Total		5.0 g

Reducing our salt intake

The NACNE and COMA guidelines suggest cutting our salt intake by about half. The following suggestions should help:

1. Reduce the amount of salt added to food during cooking – err on the side of caution by adding less than your taste demands. Salt is a taste, like sweetness, which becomes a habit. We get used to certain tastes in food and reducing the salt content will become a new habit with time. Do not be tempted to use a 'low salt' alternative as by cutting down on sodium another chemical will be added. This could bring further problems in the future.

2. Use herbs and spices to add a new dimension to the taste of food, and do not forget that freshly ground black pepper adds an excellent flavour.

3. Stop adding salt at the table – many people add salt to their food before they have even tasted it.

4. Try to limit the quantity of manufactured foods eaten as these all contain salt. The high-salt foods are bacon, processed meats such as beefburgers and sausages, smoked fish, cheese, crisps, salted peanuts and manufactured savoury products.

How can these guidelines be used by the chef? The four points apply to any catering establishment but they are worth expanding upon:

---

1. Measure the amount of salt added to the cooking water for vegetables. Instead of putting handfuls of salt into a boiler, try limiting the number or using a smaller measure such as a small spoon.

2. Most chefs are very conscious of the flavouring of a dish and recognize how crucial this is in the acceptability of a food. The skill lies in not over-seasoning and erring on the side of caution by adding slightly less, which can help lower the salt content of a dish. Using herbs and spices and experimenting with different flavours can bring about a new dimension to the enjoyment of food.

3. Perhaps salt should not be available on the table for customers' use or supplied in little packets at the counter. Some chefs consider it the height of bad manners on the part of the customer to ruin a culinary creation by adding extra salt at the table! But really it is the customer's choice.

4. Careful planning should help to regulate the appearance of high-salt foods on a menu. It does not mean that bacon, ham and sausages should not be included along with other manufactured foods, but they should be 'spread out' over the week and not concentrated into one or two days. Include plenty of fruit and vegetables, which contain potassium, on the menu as it is thought this will help balance the action of sodium.

More fibre needed

Dietary fibre is a carbohydrate, but unlike sugar and starch the body cannot digest it or absorb it into the bloodstream. It may be this fact that has caused doctors, dietitians and nutritionists in the past to ignore its usefulness to our health. Its importance has been highlighted by comparing the western diet with that of Third World countries, where dietary fibre plays a more prominent part, and studying the difference in various medical conditions between them.

Dietary fibre has been found to have many uses as far as maintaining good health is concerned. It plays a vital role in keeping our digestive tract working properly and preventing conditions such as constipation, diverticulitis and cancer of the bowel. It also helps in weight reduction and the control of diabetes, and may help prevent heart disease.

Plants are the sole suppliers of dietary fibre and the main food contributors are vegetables, fruits, cereals and cereal products. Animals and animal products contain no dietary fibre. **Our intake of dietary fibre should be between 30 g and 40 g per day** but the average intake in Britain is about 15 g to 20 g per day. This amount is made up mainly from vegetables and fruit, with little coming from cereal and cereal products.

The reason for this lack of cereal fibre is that the cereals we consume are refined. One of the results of the industrial revolution in Britain in the 18th and 19th centuries was the development of a number of processes which could change food – perhaps the start of the food-manufacturing industry. These changes led to a faster processing of foods to help provide for a growing population. For example, the development of methods of milling flour in bulk helped supply the growing demand for more flour for bread-making. Soon it was found that by adding finer sieves to the process, a lighter flour could be obtained which produced a dough resulting in a well-risen, fine-textured bread more acceptable to the public. Thus white flour was produced in quantity, replacing the wholemeal flour previously used.

To manufacture white flour from wheat, all the outer husk containing the dietary fibre is removed, along with most of the vitamins and minerals. This process results in what is termed a **refined cereal**. Wholemeal flour is made from the whole grain of the wheat; it contains the dietary fibre and is not subjected to lengthy processing. This is known as an **unrefined cereal**. Thus products made from white flour are known as refined cereal products while those made from wholemeal flour are known as unrefined cereal products. We have taken flour as an example, probably because we eat so many products made from it – bread, pasta, cakes and biscuits – but there are other cereals that are similarly processed to form refined cereals: white polished rice (both long and short grain) and breakfast cereals such as cornflakes, Rice Krispies, Ready Brek and Special K. Alternative unrefined products are wholegrain rice, wholemeal pasta, wholemeal bread, digestive biscuits, Ryvita, oat biscuits, wholemeal crackers, porridge, Weetabix, Shredded Wheat, puffed wheat and the bran cereals – this last group made from the discarded husks produced by the refining of cereals!

Over the years the people of Britain have included many refined cereals and refined cereal products in their diet, and the unrefined ones have been largely ignored. Consequently, a whole area of dietary fibre has been lacking in the diet. Studies have shown that it is the fibre from these sources, rather than vegetables and fruits, which has an impact on our digestive system. This could explain the reason behind the high incidence of digestive tract diseases in Britain. In recent years this trend for refined cereals has changed as we have as a nation become more aware of the importance of dietary fibre to good health.

Increasing our fibre intake

The following guidelines give suggestions as to how we can increase our intake of dietary fibre:

1. Eat wholemeal or granary bread (made from a mixture of wheat and rye flours). If the flavour of these breads does not appeal, have a high-fibre white bread.

2. Use wholemeal flour instead of white flour for making various products such as pastry, cakes and biscuits, or as a thickening agent in sauces.

3. Change to a wholegrain or bran-enriched breakfast cereal.

4. Use wholemeal pasta and wholegrain (brown) rice.

5. Eat plenty of fruit and vegetables, especially potatoes.

6. Try to include pulses such as peas, beans and lentils in your diet. Baked beans are cheap, nutritious and high in fibre.

7. It is important to include dietary fibre, particularly the cereal fibres, regularly in the daily diet – not just once a day but throughout the day at as many of the meals as possible. This will have the maximum beneficial effect on the digestive system. But if your diet is lacking in this type of dietary fibre, start slowly by introducing the cereal fibre at one meal only the first day and gradually building up until each meal is covered. This will prevent any adverse effects of excessive flatulence!

It is worth noting here that it is not advisable to use unprocessed bran sprinkled on food as a way of increasing cereal fibre in the diet. It is much more beneficial to follow the advice given above. Unprocessed bran should only be used on the advice of a dietitian.

If the required target of 30–40 g of dietary fibre a day is to be reached, this would mean eating, spread over all your meals:

    4–6 slices of wholemeal bread
    1 bowl of wholegrain or bran breakfast cereal
    1 large jacket potato (plus the jacket!)
    1 helping of a green vegetable
    1 helping of a root vegetable *or* 1 helping of a pulse vegetable
    2–3 portions of fruit

What can the caterer do to implement these guidelines?

1. He/she could offer a selection of breads to the customer – this will cater for all needs.

2. Substituting wholemeal flour for white for all occasions is not practical. A white sauce looks strange made with wholemeal flour! However, there are times when wholemeal flour can be used as a thickening agent and many times when the use of wholemeal flour can add a whole new dimension to the flavour of a dish. For example, using wholemeal flour in an apple crumble gives a pleasant, nutty flavour to the dish. Wholemeal flour can also be used for making Yorkshire puddings, cakes and biscuits.

   Pastry made totally from 100 per cent wholemeal flour can produce a heavy, tough product. The absorption rate of wholemeal flour is higher than for white flour and the resulting pastry can be heavy. Using a 50/50 mix brings better results, while also introducing fibre to the pastry. Many people find this pastry better for savoury dishes than for sweet ones.

3. It is always advisable to offer a good selection of cereals for breakfast, but try to concentrate on the ones which will supply plenty of dietary fibre – muesli, porridge, bran cereals, Weetabix, wheat flakes, puffed wheat and shredded wheat.

4. Using wholemeal pasta and wholegrain rice in dishes will greatly enhance the fibre content and will probably go unnoticed by your customers! The cooking time of wholemeal pasta is no different to that of white but wholegrain rice takes twice as long to cook as white rice.

5. Dietary fibre cannot be destroyed by cooking, only by being discarded in preparation. So fresh, frozen, canned or dried vegetables and fruits all contain dietary fibre. By serving jacket potatoes on a menu, you will ensure that as much dietary fibre as possible is retained. This applies also to fruits such as apples and pears.

6. All pulses are rich in dietary fibre, and there are some very tasty dishes which include beans, such as bean goulash, chilli con carne, lentil soup and aduki bean soup to name just a few. Including beans and other pulses on a menu is economical and is a useful way of providing a vegetarian dish, but it is also an excellent way of including fibre in the diet.

7. Check through the menu for each meal offered – breakfast, mid-morning, lunch, afternoon tea and dinner – to ensure that cereal fibre as well as other sources of fibre are available.

Catering for sensible eating

These practical guidelines on how to implement healthy eating policies, as recommended by the NACNE and COMA reports, are aimed at both the individual and the caterer. It is hoped that they show that what is termed 'healthy eating' is only an adaptation of a normal diet. This form of eating involves foods which we regularly include in our diets, not any special foods bought from specialist shops. Perhaps the preparation and cooking of these foods is more varied but this sensible eating should not mean radical changes or an increase in expense.

So how should the chef and caterer respond to these concepts of healthy eating? Some consider that they are only relevant to institutional catering for hospitals, residential homes or schools. Wherever the catering establishment is providing all the meals for the customer, then the nutritional needs must be met and sensible eating is a part of this. But it is just as important to provide this in *all* catering establishments, whether hotels, restaurants, fast-food outlets, luncheon clubs, industrial canteens, colleges, coffee bars or public houses, so that customers can make informed choices.

This does not necessarily mean that the whole menu should be totally based on healthy eating concepts, but it does mean that they should be represented. So the menu should include a variety of dishes from which the customer can make such a choice. The caterer and the chef, no matter what their establishment, have the responsibility of providing a choice in the menu which will allow customers to eat healthily if they want to. Appendix III provides a quick checklist to help the caterer to decide if a menu fulfils this criterion.

Checksheet

Try to answer the following questions.

1. Give three reasons why it is advisable to cut down the sugar content of our diet.
  a.
  b.
  c.

2. List three steps caterers can take to limit the sugar intake of their customers.
  a.
  b.
  c.

3. Saturated fats encourage the liver to over-produce _____.

4. Explain why high levels of cholesterol in the blood can increase the risk of heart disease.

5. List six foods containing saturated fats.
   a.   *d.*
   b.   *e.*
   c.   *f.*

6. Name four cheeses which have a fat content of 30 per cent or over.
   a.   *c.*
   b.   *d.*

7. Give three suggestions of how a caterer can reduce the fat content of a menu.
   a.
   b.
   c.

8. Which list of foods naturally contains sodium?
   a. vegetables, cereals, fruit, eggs
   b. eggs, milk, cereals, meat
   c. eggs, meat, milk, fish
   d. fruit, meat, vegetables, fish.

9. How much salt does the body require each day?

10. Give three suggestions as to how the salt content of a menu can be reduced.
   a.
   b.
   c.

11. How much dietary fibre should we have in our diet each day?

12. List four foods which could be included on a restaurant menu to increase the dietary fibre content of the meal.
   a.
   b.
   c.
   d.

Now turn to the text to check your answers.

Further study

Complete the following tasks.

1. Produce a questionnaire to put to fellow students to determine how much the message of healthy eating has affected their lives.

2. If you have a student canteen, do a survey of the foods available and find out whether it is possible to choose foods which comply with nutritional guidelines.

3. Plan and produce a three-course luncheon menu, with choices, for the training restaurant, which comply with nutritional guidelines.

4. Produce a questionnaire to present to customers after they have tasted the meals served in Task 3! You could include questions on their opinion of the meal – taste, colour, presentation – and on their opinions about healthy eating.

5. Investigate the range of low-fat products available to the consumer. Set up a tasting panel to determine the acceptability of these products.

6. Produce a number of samples of a dish with:
   a. no salt added
   b. small quantities of salt added
   c. enough salt to suit your taste
   d. too much salt added.
   Set up a tasting panel to try out the dishes and monitor the response.

7. Plan and produce a dish which will help you compare the difference in cooking time, appearance, taste and acceptability of (a) wholemeal pasta and (b) white pasta. The exercise can be repeated using brown rice and white rice.

Catering for different diets

This chapter will try to explain the principles behind a number of different types of diet. These fall into two main categories – moral/religious diets and special diets. It is important that caterers understand the needs of those concerned. In Britain, more people than ever before are eating away from home and using a variety of catering establishments either out of necessity or as part of their social life. This includes people who for reasons of choice, religion or medical necessity have to follow a certain pattern of eating. It is very important that the chef can cater for all different types of diet.

Moral and religious diets

The vegetarian diet

A vegetarian diet excludes all meat and meat products and also fish. This includes any products which are obtained by the killing of an animal. Vegetarians can be divided into **ovo-vegetarians**, who eat eggs but no dairy produce, **lacto-vegetarians**, who eat dairy produce but no eggs, **lacto-ovo-vegetarians**, who eat both eggs and dairy produce, and **vegans**, who eat neither. The reasons for following this type of diet are many and include:

Religious reasons
Many of the world's religions forbid the eating of flesh in their dietary laws. Orthodox Hindus and Buddhists forbid the eating of animals.

Moral reasons
A growing number of people consider our modern methods of farming and fishing to be inhumane. Many also consider that the worldwide shortage of food, particularly of animal foods, could be solved if more people were vegetarians.

Personal reasons
Some individuals cannot tolerate the taste and flavour of meat and fish. Some people find they are allergic to meat and meat products and although they cannot be strictly termed true vegetarians, many of these non-meat eaters follow a vegetarian diet.

Health reasons
A vegetarian diet is thought by some to be more beneficial to health, because it avoids the saturated, animal fat of meat and fish. It is worth pointing out here, however, that a vegetarian diet that includes dairy products and eggs can still be high in fats as these foods also contain animal fat.

FOODS ALLOWED

Eggs	Cream	Vegetable oils
Milk – all types	Margarine	All vegetables
Yogurt	Nuts and seeds	Pulses
Vegetarian cheese	Textured vegetable protein (TVP)	All fruits
Butter	Cereals and cereal products	Most drinks
Tofu	Agar or vegetarian jelly	Jams and preserves

FOODS AVOIDED

Meat – all types
Poultry and game – all types
Fish – all types
Shellfish
Lard, dripping, suet
Bone stocks and fish stocks
Gravies and meat extracts
All manufactured foods containing the above
Gelatin, aspic, jelly (extracted from animal bones)
Ice cream made from animal fat
Cheese made with rennet

Most of the cheeses available to us are made with the enzyme rennet, which is extracted from the stomachs of calves. This is unacceptable for many vegetarians so it is very important that any cheese dishes used as a vegetarian choice are made with a vegetarian cheese which does not involve the use of rennet, or with cottage cheese or some of the curd cheeses. Many vegetarians also prefer to eat free-range eggs in preference to the battery-farmed varieties. Caffeine is also avoided by many vegetarians as it is a stimulant. So decaffeinated coffee and herbal teas should be offered as an alternative.

Cooking methods

These do not vary from normal, except that vegetable oils must be used for deep-fat frying, shallow frying and roasting. Vegetable fats/oils must also be used for sealing foods. The fat/oil should be fresh: do not use any fat or oil in which meat or fish has been cooked. (N.B. Fried foods should be kept to a minimum.)

Recipes

Adaptation of recipes to avoid lard, suet and all animal white fats is essential. Agar jelly or vegetarian jelly should be used in recipes as a substitute for gelatin or aspic. Vegetarian cheese and decaffeinated coffee can be used as substitutes for cheese and coffee respectively.

A balanced diet

As with all diets, a correct balance of nutrients is essential. A vegetarian can become deficient in iron and vitamin B12 and may need supplements. A menu must be planned to give a balance of all the nutrients:

Proteins

The main sources are eggs, milk, yogurt, fromage frais and cheese, but the use of pulses, nuts and cereals will supplement the protein intake. Soya beans and its products – soya bean flour and textured vegetable protein (TVP) – will enhance the HBV (high biological value) protein intake. However, meat-flavoured TVP will not normally be acceptable to a vegetarian, and only unflavoured should be used.

Fats

Use only butter, vegetable oils, vegetable oil margarine/fats. Single, half-fat, whipping, double and clotted cream can be used.

Carbohydrates

All cereal and cereal products are allowed but many vegetarians prefer wholegrain cereal, wholemeal flour, pasta and bread.

Vitamins and minerals

A good variety of different vegetables, fruits and cereals will ensure an adequate supply. It is important to offer a variety of the protein foods that are permitted.

The vegan diet

This diet excludes *all* animal foods and animal products. The reasons for following this type of diet include:

Religious reasons

Some of the world's religions advocate the use of a vegan diet. Some orthodox Hindus, particularly women, as well as Buddhists and some Rastafarians, are vegans, although in some cases milk is included in the diet.

Moral reasons

The majority of vegans in Britain abhor the eating of any flesh and the rearing of animals for food. The use of milk by human beings is seen as depriving the young of that animal of food, while eating eggs is depriving a young chick of the chance to live.

Personal reasons

Many vegans consider their diet is a more healthy way of eating.

FOODS ALLOWED

Vegetables of all types
Pulses – peas, all types of beans and lentils
Fruit of all types
Nuts and seeds
Textured vegetable protein (TVP), a natural-flavoured soya bean derivative
Soya bean milk – extracted from soya beans
Tofu – a soya bean curd
Vegetable oils
Vegetable oil margarine – these must not contain whey proteins. The most suitable variety is Tomor
Cereals and cereal products – but check label to avoid additions of egg or whey proteins
All drinks (except those containing caffeine and some vegans avoid alcohol)
Agar or vegetarian jelly
Jams and preserves
Carob

FOODS AVOIDED

Meat – all types
Poultry and game – all types
Fish and shellfish
Eggs
Milk, yogurt, fromage frais
Butter and margarines, which include whey proteins
Cream – all types
Lard, suet, dripping
All manufactured foods containing animal products (look at the label)
Cheese
Bone stock and fish stock
Gravies and meat extracts
Honey – this is considered by some to be depriving a bee of food
Gelatine, jelly, chocolate

Cooking methods
These do not vary from normal except that it is essential that no animal fats are used for frying, roasting or sealing foods. Only fresh vegetable oils/fats must be used.

Recipes
If adapting conventional recipes (making pastry, for example), it must be remembered that all fats must be derived from vegetable oils. No animal milk or eggs can be used in a cake mixture, for example.

A balanced diet

The majority of vegans in Britain are very knowledgeable about their diet and are therefore aware of the need to include all the nutrients in a balanced form. However, vegans can suffer from severe iron deficiency and from lack of vitamin B12, which is only found in animal products. It may be necessary to take these nutrients in supplement form.

When planning a vegan diet it is very important to ensure a balance of all the nutrients:

Proteins

Pulses, cereals and nuts can be used as a protein source but these will only provide LBV proteins. Soya beans, tofu, soya bean milk and TVP are the only available source of HBV proteins and should be regularly included in the diet.

Fats

Use only vegetable oils and vegetable oil margarines.

Carbohydrates

As normal, but use wholegrain cereals, wholemeal breads (no animal fat added), wholegrain rice and wholegrain pasta (no eggs added).

Vitamins and minerals

It is essential to offer a good variety of vegetables, fruits and cereals, as well as the protein foods allowed, to ensure an adequate supply.

In Chapter 1 we looked briefly at the dietary laws which affect the choice of foods which followers of certain religions have to abide by. In this section we shall look at the practicalities of catering for such diets.

Jewish cookery

The majority of orthodox Jews who keep very strictly to all aspects of their religious laws will rarely eat away from their homes or from homes of other orthodox Jews. If they have to eat in a restaurant/hotel they will eat as vegetarians. However, there are a number of catering firms now who specialize in providing correctly produced cook-freeze products for a Jewish diet.

Cooking methods

These are no different from normal, except that meat and meat products must never be cooked using utensils in which milk and milk products have been cooked. In practice, this means keeping a duplicate set of all equipment to ensure this segregation. The preparation and cooking of dishes for this diet must be overviewed by a rabbi, which makes many establishments unsuitable as providers of Jewish food.

FOODS ALLOWED

Kosher meat – beef, lamb, venison, chicken, turkey, goose and duck
Round fish – with fins and scales
Milk, cheese, cream
Butter
All vegetables, including pulses
All fruits
All cereals and cereal products but check labels for animal fats
Nuts and seeds
Preserves
All drinks

FOODS AVOIDED

Meat and poultry which has not been ritually slaughtered in
compliance with dietary laws
Pork and pork products – sausages, pork pies, etc.
Flat fish, turbot
All shellfish
Caviare – the roe of an unclean fish
Eggs and milk from unclean animals and birds
Gelatin made from bones of animals
Lard

Recipes

Butter derived from milk must not be used with a meat dish so kosher
margarine or vegetable oils should be used. Similarly milk, cheese, cream,
cream cheese or ice cream must not be used on a menu where kosher
meat is included in the main course.

A balanced diet

As with any diet it is essential that a good balance of nutrients is provided:

Proteins

This will be obtained from kosher meats, permitted fish, milk and milk
products, as well as cereals, pulses, nuts and seeds. It is important that the
individual varies the protein intake to provide a good variety of both HBV
and LBV proteins.

Fats

Use kosher margarine, butter or vegetable oils.

Carbohydrates

Obtained from cereals and cereal products including unleavened bread, as
well as from some vegetables and preserves.

Vitamins and minerals

Like other diets, a good variety of different foods will ensure a good mix of
these nutrients.

If in doubt always consult the customer! They will be able to supply you with the necessary information to help cater for this diet.

Ethnic diets

The dictionary definition of ethnic is 'not native of this country'. In this respect, French, Italian and Chinese cuisine, to name but a few, are examples of ethnic cookery. It would, however, be an impossible task to cover all aspects of ethnic diets if we take this definition literally. Instead we will stick to those diets where religious laws govern the choice of foods. These include those followed by Hindus (both orthodox and non-orthodox), Sikhs, Muslims and Rastafarians. The case of Buddhists was highlighted when we examined vegetarian or vegan diets. The dietary laws of the various religions were examined in Chapter 1, so here we shall look at the practical issues. These are summarized in Table 9.1, which gives details of the foods to be avoided by each religion.

FOODS ALLOWED

Vegetables – all kinds
Pulses
Fruits
Nuts
Preserves
Cereals and cereal products

Rastafarians do not allow the use of processed foods and Muslims, like orthodox Jews, must have the animals ritually slaughtered. The meat is then termed 'halal'.

Table 9.1. **Foods to be avoided according to the main religious dietary laws**

Food	Hindus Orthodox	Hindus Non-orthodox	Sikhs	Muslims	Rastafarians
Alcohol	No	Yes	Some	No	No
Beef and offal	No	No	No	Yes*	No
Eggs	Some	Yes	Yes	Yes	No
Fish – oily	No	No	Yes	Yes	No
Fish – white	No	Yes	Yes	Yes	No
Lamb and offal	No	Yes	Yes	Yes*	No
Milk and milk products	Yes	Yes	Yes	Yes	Yes
Poultry	No	Yes	Yes	Yes*	No
Pork/lard/ham/ bacon	No	No	No	No	No
Shellfish	No	Some	Yes	No	No

*Meat must be halal.

Cooking methods
In none of the religions is there any variation from normal, but vegetable oils must be used for all types of frying, roasting and sealing.

Recipes
Adaptation of existing recipes must take into account the foods which must be avoided in each case.

A balanced diet
This is sometimes difficult to achieve where the restrictions on foods are high. For example for orthodox Hindus and Rastafarians, particularly women of child-bearing age, who are most at risk from anaemia, iron and vitamin B12 deficiency will be high. It is important to offer as wide a variety of permitted foods as possible to maximize the chance of obtaining sufficient quantities of all the necessary nutrients.

Special diets

A special diet is one which has to be followed for medical reasons, and is where a 'normal' diet is modified to help alleviate and control physical symptoms. There are a number of different types of special diet, all of which are for specific conditions. The major special diets are listed below:

*Diabetic – controls diabetes

Food allergy – controls the adverse effects of some foods

*Gluten-free – controls coeliac disease

High calcium – for avoiding osteoporosis

High fibre – prevents constipation, stimulates a 'lazy' bowel

High protein – for post-operative, burns, bedsores, replaces lost protein, generally builds up a person

*Low animal fat – reduces cholesterol levels

Low calcium – reduces calcium levels in the body, prevents kidney stones

Low fat – controls gall bladder conditions, cholecystitis, obstructive jaundice, steatorrhoea

Low fibre – rests the gut and reduces inflammation (short-term diet)

Low potassium – sometimes necessary to help in kidney failure

Low protein – for liver and kidney complaints

Low residue – rests the bowel after surgery, aids acute inflammation of the large intestine (short-term diet)

Low sodium – to reduce high sodium levels in the body, e.g. through kidney failure

Metabolic disorders in children – e.g. phenalketonuria

Milk free – for those showing allergic reactions to milk and milk products

No added salt – aids against hypertension

*Weight reduction – to aid against physical strain, e.g. back strain, varicose veins, heart disease, hiatus hernia

*Denotes those diets which will be studied in detail.

Weight reduction diets

We saw in the last chapter how, at any one time, over half the adult population of Britain is following some form of weight reduction diet. Probably this is the most well known of all the special diets and certainly the most difficult to follow. The majority of special diets will alleviate symptoms if followed – not so the weight reduction diet! After following such a diet for a day or two, you will not wake up the next morning having shed kilograms of weight or feeling much better, as to lose weight takes time, infinite patience and tremendous will power. For those of you who have never had a weight problem and are sylph-like in stature, do not scoff at those who just look at a cake and put on weight! Treat them with considerable sympathy as weight loss is, for many of them, hard work to achieve.

There are in fact a large number of different weight reduction diets, but the principle behind all of them is to reduce the person's energy intake (measured in kilocalories/kilojoules), to enable them to lose weight. The majority of diets, however, are totally unsuitable for losing more than 7 lb or 3 kg as they either do not provide a completely balanced diet or are too low in kilocalories to maintain the body's needs. Such diets as the Grapefruit Diet, the Prune Diet, the Complete Fruit Diet and the very low calorie diets fall into this category.

The diet which, in my experience, has proved to be most successful for those with the right motivation to lose weight is one that is **low in fat**, **low in sugar** and **high in fibre**. This diet is for the long-term overweight – those people who have more than 7 kg or 1 stone to lose, and it will ensure weight loss while maintaining good health for the body.

Fat is the most concentrated energy source for the body and, along with sugar, can form the major source of energy in our diet. By reducing these two nutrients and maintaining the same level of protein a low-kilocalorie/kilojoule diet can be achieved. The intake should be around 1000–1500 kcal per day (4200–5300 kJ). Such a diet should have the consent of the individual's doctor and be monitored by a professional person such as a dietitian.

There are two main reason for going on this diet:

Medical reasons
This is by far the most important reason. Excessive weight can put enormous strain on the body, causing varicose veins, back strain and hiatus hernia. It can also aggravate arthritis, hypertension (high blood pressure) and increase the possibility of heart disease and strokes.

Social image
Advertising encourages individuals to aim for a 'slim figure' to enhance attractiveness. This is really an impossible goal for the majority of us as it takes no account of height and bone structure.

FOODS ALLOWED

Lean meat, particularly chicken, turkey, rabbit, offal
Fish, particularly white fish
Small quantities of eggs and low-fat cheese
Cottage cheese
All vegetables, including potatoes
All types of fresh fruit and fruit canned in natural/apple juice
Low-fat spreads – small quantities
Semi-skimmed or skimmed milk
Natural low-fat yogurt or fromage frais, occasional fruit yogurt
Wholemeal bread (4 large slices per day) and crispbreads
Wholemeal pasta and wholegrain rice
Wholegrain breakfast cereals, e.g. Weetabix, shredded wheat, porridge oats, bran cereals, puffed wheat
Tea, coffee, unsweetened fruit juices, low-calorie fizzy drinks and low-calorie squashes
Soups and low-calorie sauce (made with skimmed milk and cornflour)
Fruit purée used as a preserve
Dry wines and sherries
Herbs, spices, vinegar, vinegar pickles

FOODS AVOIDED

Fried foods – deep and shallow fried
Cheese, cream, nuts, crisps, corn snacks
Chips, roast potatoes
Fatty meats, fried fish
Whole milk, condensed and evaporated milk, milk substitutes
Chocolate, snack bars
Sugar as a sweetener, sweets – all types
Jam, honey, marmalade, syrup, treacle
Desserts with a high sugar content
Cakes, gâteaux, sweet biscuits, pastry
Fruit squashes, fizzy drinks, sweet wines, beers, spirits

The question of body size and the ease or otherwise of gaining weight is a problem that has vexed the experts for decades and continues to do so. You must know of people who can eat whatever they like and still be like two boards put together, while others simply look at a cake and the weight goes on! What causes this difference is not understood although many theories have been put forward in explanation. It seems likely that genetic make-up plays a part, but scientists are still pondering the problem. Until they discover the answer we are left with the only solution – weight reduction diets.

Cooking methods

Deep-fat frying, shallow frying and sealing *must* be avoided. Grilling, stewing, poaching, braising, casseroling, boiling, steaming and microwave cooking are all suitable methods. Glazing of vegetables with butter or margarine must be avoided.

Recipes

As much fat and sugar must be cut out of this diet as possible, so choose recipes which can easily be adapted to suit. Sugar should not be used as a sweetener, but artificial sweeteners can be used as a substitute. High-fat recipes must be avoided and no cream added to soups and sauces. Natural yogurt and/or fromage frais may be used as substitutes for cream in some recipes. It is the dessert part of the menu which will tax the skills of most chefs as the variety of dishes for this diet is limited. Colour and presentation are very important to make the meals as attractive as possible.

A balanced diet

Although the energy intake is lowered in this diet so that the individual will use up their stores of excess fat, it is essential to maintain a good balance of the nutrients to ensure good health as weight is lost. Providing a variety of different meats, fish, vegetables, cereals and fruit will ensure a balanced and interesting diet.

Low animal fat diet

This diet has been widely used in the past 20 years to reduce cholesterol levels in the blood so as to help prevent high blood pressure and heart disease. It involves the elimination of as much animal fat in the diet as possible. The term 'animal fat' is somewhat misleading as people who follow this diet are encouraged to cut down their total fat intake, whether from animal or vegetable sources. Very small amounts of fat are allowed, but these must come from vegetable and fish sources only. This diet also encourages a reduction in those foods which contain cholesterol. In my view, this latter step is not as important as the lowering of the fat content of the diet. As long as the cholesterol-containing foods do not appear on a regular daily basis, small quantities of these foods should not make a significant difference to blood cholesterol levels. This diet should also be high in fibre, particularly from cereal sources.

FOODS ALLOWED

Chicken, turkey, small quantities of lean beef, pork and lamb
Rabbit, occasional offal – liver, kidney
Fish – all types, especially oily fish*
Shellfish – not more than once a week
Low-fat spreads if really required and small quantities of pure
vegetable oils and soft vegetable oil margarines
Skimmed or semi-skimmed milk, low-fat yogurt or fromage frais,
cottage cheese, occasionally low-fat cheese
All cereals but particularly wholemeal flour, wholemeal bread,
wholemeal pasta, brown rice and wholegrain breakfast cereals
Crispbreads and plain biscuits, digestive biscuits
All fruit
All vegetables
Occasionally, pastry and cakes made with vegetable fats only
All drinks
Jam, preserves and boiled sweets
Sorbet
Herbs, spices, vinegar, vinegar pickles
Nuts and seeds – limited amounts

FOODS AVOIDED

Fat on meat, fatty meats – streaky bacon, belly pork, breast of lamb
Canned meat, duck, goose, meat products
Whole milk, condensed and evaporated milk, cream – all types
Eggs, cheese
Butter, lard, suet, block margarine, blended vegetable oils
Pies, pastries and all commercial cakes
Cream biscuits, chocolate biscuits, crisps
Lemon curd, marzipan, salad oils/dressings
Chocolate/chocolates, toffee, fudge, butterscotch
Dairy ice cream
Fried foods

---

*Recent studies have shown that including oily fish regularly in the weekly diet can help prevent heart disease.

Most people who go on this diet suffer from hyperlipidaemia, which is the medical term used to describe a high level of fatty substances (lipids) circulating in the blood. The best-known of these substances is cholesterol, a substance essential to the body and manufactured in the liver. Animal fats (saturated fats) are known to increase the production of cholesterol in the body. The relationship between dietary fat and cholesterol levels and the effect of high cholesterol levels in the blood has been explained in detail in Chapter 8, in the section 'Fats and heart disease'.

This diet has also been promoted as a preventive measure to combat heart disease in the population as a whole.

Some customers following this diet may also restrict their sugar and starch intake. It is therefore important to consult the individual if there is any doubt, before cutting down the carbohydrate content of the meals offered.

Cooking methods
Fried foods should be strictly limited on this diet and where necessary only pure vegetable oils are used for sealing foods. All other cooking methods are acceptable.

Recipes
When adapting recipes for this diet, only pure vegetable fats/margarine must be used as a substitute for butter, block margarine, lard and suet. But it must be emphasized that the principle of the diet is to cut down total fat as much as possible so fried foods, pastry, cakes and gâteaux should be strictly limited. The use of wholegrain cereals in recipes is also encouraged.

A balanced diet
A good variety of the foods allowed should be offered to ensure an adequate supply of all the nutrients. Good quantities of high-fibre carbohydrates should be included to ensure adequate energy intake to counteract the drop in fat intake.

Diabetic diet

This diet is prescribed by a doctor for a person who is suffering from the disease diabetes mellitus. **It involves a controlled carbohydrate diet which is low in fat content and high in dietary fibre**. Each diabetic will have a diet specifically designed for their personal needs by a dietitian and this will form an essential part of the treatment and control of the condition. It is extremely important that a diabetic follows the diet at all times.

A description of the condition diabetes was given in Chapter 8, in the section 'Sugar versus our teeth, our weight and our health', so it will suffice to just summarize the major points here. Diabetes is caused by the body failing to produce any or enough of the hormone, insulin, which controls the glucose levels in the blood. Lack of insulin will result in dangerously high levels of glucose in the blood, which, if left untreated, will prove fatal. There are two types of diabetes. Type 1 or insulin-dependent diabetes occurs when no insulin is produced by the body. People suffering from this condition must inject themselves daily with insulin and follow a specific diet. Type 2 or non-insulin dependent diabetes occurs when the body is producing insufficient or sporadic quantities of insulin. People suffering from this must follow a specific diet and may also be required to take tablets to encourage the pancreas to produce more insulin.

If the person also has a weight problem, the diabetes is controlled with the help of a weight reduction diet, as described above, which will alleviate the symptoms of diabetes as well as help weight loss.

When dietitians are developing a diabetic diet, they will first discover the normal food intake of their patients before they developed the disease. From this information it will be possible to determine the carbohydrate intake as well as the general eating pattern. Taking into account the weight of their patients, as well as their occupations and lifestyles, they are able to develop a diet that is specific to each patient's needs.

The diet will cut out some carbohydrate foods, especially sugar, and limit the person to a certain quantity of starch-based foods per day to suit their needs. This, in conjunction with a low fat intake and high dietary fibre, will control the symptoms of diabetes. Obviously other factors are taken into account, such as whether the person has to inject themselves with insulin or not. Dietitians will carefully instruct their patients on how to cope with this diet. So when catering for this type of diet, the chef should always consult his/her diabetic customer to ensure that the dishes supplied are suitable.

Cooking methods
All methods of cooking are allowed but frying foods should be avoided. Butter or margarine should not be added to vegetables and cream should be avoided in soups and sauces.

Recipes
Sugar must *not* be used to sweeten any foods but artificial sweeteners can be added. All starch-based ingredients should be accurately weighed when making a dish. Most diabetics can include the occasional pastry, plain cake or scone mix in their diet but check with the customer first. Use vegetable oil/fats rather than butter.

There are a number of diabetic cookbooks available, although these may need adapting from home use to catering. The British Diabetic Association can help with any queries and their address can be found at the back of the book.

A balanced diet
Diabetics follow the diet calculated for them and they will need to eat a certain amount of carbohydrate foods at each meal. It is important that the quantity of carbohydrate is kept to, that it is high in dietary fibre and that the fat intake is kept low. Always check with the customer to obtain correct quantities of carbohydrate foods.

It is very important that the meals are nutritionally balanced and a good variety of the foods allowed on this diet will help to ensure this.

FOODS ALLOWED

Lean meat	Tomatoes, carrots, swedes
Poultry	Turnips, beans, peas
Fish	Grapefruit, gooseberries
Bacon – lean	Melon, rhubarb
Tinned meats	Red/blackcurrants
Eggs – small amounts	Tea/coffee
Green vegetables	Low-calorie drinks – lemonade, other fizzy
Baked beans, sweetcorn	drinks, squashes
	Fruit juices

Salt, pepper, herbs, spices, vinegar, vinegar pickles, Bovril, Marmite, and soups can all be included in the diet.

FOODS TO INCLUDE ON A DAILY BASIS

The following foods must be included in the diet each day and specific amounts will be stated on the diabetic's diet sheet.

Fruit – fresh fruit or fruit canned in its own juice or apple juice, dried fruits
Fats – use butter and margarine sparingly
Bread – use wholemeal bread
Cereals – use wholegrain breakfast cereals, wholemeal pasta and brown rice
Flour – use wholemeal flour in place of white flour
Potatoes – jacket, boiled, steamed, mashed, savoury dishes with stock
Milk – use skimmed or semi-skimmed, low-fat natural yogurt, low-fat/low-sugar flavoured yogurt, low-fat ice cream or sorbet

FOODS AVOIDED

Sugar	Fruit canned in syrup	Bitter lemon,
Glucose	Manufactured fruit pies/tarts/gâteaux	lemonade
Lactose	Iced or cream-filled cakes	Tonic water
Sweets	Buttercream-filled cakes	Fizzy drinks
Chocolates	Packet desserts	Lucozade
Jams	Chocolate biscuits	Ribena
Honey	Sweet biscuits	Fruit squashes
Marmalade	Sugar-coated breakfast cereals	Sweet wines
Syrup	Sweetened muesli	Sweet sherries
Lemon curd	Cream	Beers/lagers
All fried foods		Fatty meats

Alcohol, such as spirits, diet lagers, dry wine or dry sherries, is allowed in moderation.
Artificial sweeteners can be used as a substitute for sugar.
Diabetic foods are not necessary on this diet.

Gluten-free diet

This diet is prescribed for people who have an allergy to gluten. Gluten is a protein produced when wheat or rye flour is mixed with a liquid. In fact it is made up of two proteins called gliadin and glutenin: when mixed with a liquid they form an elasticated substance which makes gluten so useful in bread-making and confectionery. Gluten is found in small quantities in barley and oats, but rice and maize do not contain it.

In Chapter 4, we discussed how the food we eat is digested and absorbed. The inner lining of the small intestine, which is where food is absorbed across the gut wall and into the bloodstream, is made up of tiny finger-like projections called villi. These villi help to increase the surface area of absorption, allowing maximum quantities of nutrients to pass into the body.

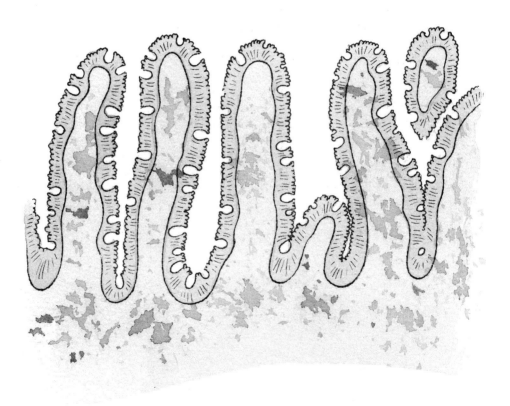

Figure 9.1 A cross-section of the lining of the normal jejunum with its long, finger-shaped villi (× 130)

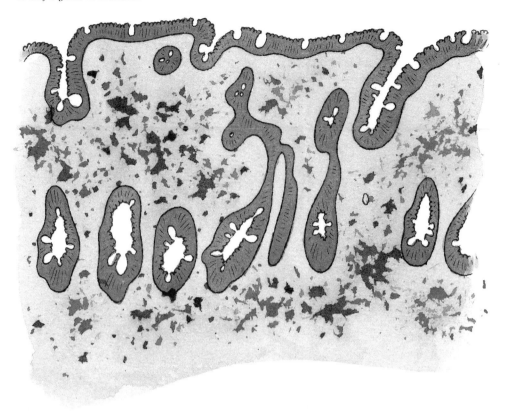

Figure 9.2 The intestinal mucosa of a patient with untreated coeliac disease. The surface is almost flat, with only the remnants of villi to be seen ($\times 130$).

For some people the gluten present in cereal foods acts as an irritant to the small intestine and badly damages the villi, virtually wiping them out. This can best be illustrated using a diagram, and Figure 9.1 shows a normal small intestine with visible villi, whereas Figure 9.2 shows a small intestine where the villi have been flattened due to gluten intolerance. This condition is known as **coeliac disease** and it is not fully understood what actually causes the intolerance to gluten to occur. It is more common in children and teenagers but it can also occur in adults. It is treated by using a gluten-free diet. If untreated the person suffers from malabsorption with symptoms of severe loss of weight, diarrhoea and vitamin/mineral deficiencies.

Many manufactured foods are free of gluten and most main food manufacturers can supply a list of their gluten-free products. Further information on such products can also be obtained from the Coeliac Society, the address of which can be found at the back of this book.

FOODS ALLOWED

Beef, lamb, pork, offal, rabbit, venison
Chicken, turkey, duck, goose and game birds
Bacon, ham
Eggs
Milk – all types, cream, cheese
Fresh fish and shellfish, fish canned in oil/water
Pulses – peas, beans, lentils
Fruit – all types
Vegetables – fresh, frozen, dried, canned in water/brine
Home-made soups with no wheat flour/barley added
Cereals – gluten-free products, rice, sago, tapioca, cornflour, buckwheat, millet, arrowroot, potato flour, soya flour, rice flour, split pea flour, cornflakes, Rice Krispies
Gelatine, jelly
Butter, lard, margarine, vegetable oils, fresh suet
Nuts, sugar, jam, honey, marmalade, syrup
Fresh/dried herbs and spices
Yeast, gluten-free baking powder
Tea, coffee, fruit juice, squashes, fizzy drinks
Spirits, wines, fortified wines, cider, liqueurs

FOODS AVOIDED

Any meats cooked with flour or breadcrumbs, meat pies/pasties, sausage rolls, *sausages, *beefburgers, *canned meats, *pâtés, *meat pastes
Fish cooked in batter and breadcrumbs, fish fingers, fishcakes, fish canned in sauce
*Yogurt, *synthetic cream, *cheese spreads, *processed cheese
Wheat, barley, rye, semolina, wheat flour, wheatbran, wheatgerm
Bread, crispbreads, cakes and biscuits
All pasta and the majority of breakfast cereals, *baby cereals, *infant foods
Fruit pie fillings, fruit pies, *baked beans, *instant potato, *crisps
*Canned and packet soups, *canned milk puddings, *ice cream, *mousses
*Custard powder, *cake decorations, *cooking chocolate, *dessert mixes
Gâteaux, cakes, pastry
*Packet suet, *peanut butter, *dry roasted peanuts
*Curry powder, *mustard, *stock cubes, *gravy mixes and browning
*Sauces, *salad dressings, *chutneys and pickles
*Sweets, *chocolate, *mincemeat, *lemon curd
*Beef and chicken essence, *milk shake flavourings
*Drinking chocolate, *cocoa
*Beer and lager

*Indicates that some brands are gluten-free.

Some gluten-free products can be obtained on prescription for someone suffering from coeliac disease, including gluten-free flour, bread, pasta, biscuits and crispbreads. These are made using wheat starch with the proteins removed. These products are not available for the chef/caterer but if coeliac customers are 'regulars' or staying in a hotel, at a conference or college, they will be able to supply these products to supplement the meals.

Cooking methods

These do not vary from normal and all cooking methods can be used. Remember not to flour or crumb foods with wheat flour before frying/sealing.

Recipes

All recipes which contain wheat/rye flour or products made with these *must* be avoided. Even a small quantity of gluten can cause severe reactions to a coeliac. Sauces can be thickened with cornflour or egg.

There really is no substitute for wheat flour when it comes to producing bread, pastry and cakes. Gluten helps provide the light texture in such products. Wheat starch, which has the protein removed, rice flour, potato flour and cornflour will not produce the same effect even with a raising agent. Producing acceptable gluten-free products will tax the culinary skills of the chef! However, do not be deterred as practice does make perfect products. There are some useful cookery books available which will help and the Coeliac Society can provide some tested recipes.

A balanced diet

As for any diet, a good variety of permitted foods needs to be included on a menu to ensure an adequate supply of nutrients. A coeliac needs to come to terms with gluten-free cereals as early in their treatment as possible, so as to provide sufficient supplies of starch-based carbohydrate. They should not rely on sugars and fats as energy sources.

The big problem in this diet is the lack of dietary fibre from cereal sources. Fruit and vegetables will supply the main source but plenty of pulse-based foods – peas, beans and lentils – will help.

Only four special diets have been highlighted in this chapter, and these were included because they are the most common diets the chef/caterer will have to cater for. Further information about these and all other special diets can be obtained from the British Dietetic Association, whose address can be found at the back of this book. Each district health authority employs dietitians who will be more than willing to supply further information on any diet which needs to be catered for. They can be contacted at the local hospital. However, customers following special diets will gladly supply firsthand information about their diet.

Checksheet

Try to answer the following questions.

1. Explain the difference between a vegetarian and vegan diet.

2. List three protein foods a vegan can eat.
 a.   *b.*   *c.*

3. What alternatives to the following foods are there for a vegetarian to eat:
 a. cheese
 b. gelatin
 c. coffee
 d. lard

4. State the reasons why someone may follow a vegan diet.
 a.
 b.

5. What major effect does cooking Jewish food have on the organization of a kitchen?

6. List four foods which are allowed by the dietary laws of the Hindu, Sikh, Muslim and Rastafarian religions.
 a.   *c.*
 b.   *d.*

7. A person who is trying to lose weight should follow a diet low in _____ and _____ and high in _____ .

8. Which list of foods should be avoided on a weight reduction diet?
 a. potatoes, cream, sugar
 b. potatoes, apples, fried foods
 c. cream, fried foods, sugar
 d. cream, fried foods, potatoes.

9. Give an alternative food which a person following a low animal fat diet could eat.
 a. butter:
 b. cream:
 c. belly pork:
 d. whole milk:
 e. fried fish and chips:

10. List four foods a diabetic must avoid.
 a.   *c.*
 b.   *d.*

11. Which two proteins is gluten made up of?
   a. gliadin, caesinogen
   b. gliadin, glutenin
   c. gliadin, gelatin
   d. glutenin, gelatin

12. Name four foods which contain gluten.
   a.   *c.*
   b.   *d.*

Now turn to the text to check your answers.

Further study

Complete the following tasks.

1. Many of the world's religions have important religious festivals. Research the major festivals of the following religions, stating any special foods which are eaten at that time.
   a. Jewish
   b. Hindu
   c. Sikh
   d. Muslim

2. Collect menus from a number of catering establishments – restaurants, hotels, luncheon clubs, fast-food outlets – and establish how many of them cater for the following diets:
   a. vegetarian
   b. vegan
   c weight reduction
   d. diabetic
   e. gluten-free

3. What ingredients would you substitute in a recipe for cheesecake, if you were preparing this for a weight reduction diet?

4. Plan and produce a three-course luncheon menu for a restaurant for each of the following special diets:
   a. weight reduction
   b. diabetic
   c. low animal fat
   d. gluten-free

5. Describe three dessert dishes which would be suitable for someone following a diabetic diet.

ten

Menu planning

In this last chapter we shall concentrate on the criteria for menu planning, and relate it to the practicalities of various catering establishments, and the needs of different groups within the community. Obviously our priority in this book has been nutrition and how it relates to the work of the chef/caterer, but this cannot be dealt with in isolation and must be thought of as an integral part of the general planning of menus and of kitchen organization.

Basic criteria for planning a menu

Every caterer has his/her own set of criteria when faced with planning a menu. The following ideas are based on a number of years of experience, and should be considered when setting out to plan a menu. There is no significance in the order of priority – each point is of equal weighting.

Needs of the customer

What type of customer are you attracting? Are they young, middle-aged, elderly or a mixture of ages? Are they office workers, business men and women, factory workers, tourists or students? These are important considerations and they will determine the type of service required and the projected turnover of the business as well as the sort of meals/snacks required.

Type of service

Is it a self-service establishment, cafeteria, silver service or family service? Again these are important considerations as some dishes may not lend themselves to silver or family service.

Budget

A vital component when planning a menu. Every establishment will have some form of budget to keep within. This budget will not just cover food costs, but will also take into account overheads such as rent, business tax, services and staff costs. But budgets vary with the type of establishment: a top-class restaurant can afford to airlift food from all over the world throughout the year as the customers are prepared and able to pay for such luxuries, whereas a council-run residential home for the elderly will have a very limited budget to cover food costs.

Availability of staff

Catering is a fluid market as far as staff are concerned, with chefs and ancillary staff moving jobs frequently. Unsocial hours, split duties and low pay all add to the problem. It is no use planning a complex menu if there is a lack of staff to produce it!

Ability of staff

How experienced are they and what are their qualifications? What are their capabilities? It is no use producing a menu requiring skills from an advanced catering course if the staff have qualifications from a basic skills course! The menu must reflect the capabilities of the staff.

Availability of equipment

This, too, is an important point. It is no good planning for a number of dishes if there is insufficient equipment available to prepare or cook them. It is difficult to produce one hundred portions of jacket potatoes if there is only one small oven available. The menu must include dishes which can be readily catered for using both small and large equipment.

Availability of raw materials

The use of foods in season is important in menu planning. However, with modern transport and air freight, it is now possible to obtain seasonal foods all the year round and sometimes at a reasonable price. The availability of a wide range of foods for all consumers has increased enormously over the past decade, with exotic fruits and vegetables appearing on supermarket shelves. But it is still good practice to use foods, especially fruit and vegetables, when they are in season or when there is a glut on the market, as the price will be more favourable. Some foods, such as game birds, should only appear on a menu at certain times of the year when shooting is allowed.

Different methods of cooking

Incorporating as many different and varied methods of cooking is important in menu planning. It helps to prevent repetitions and similarities in dishes. In Britain we tend to include a lot of fried dishes on our menus. This method of cooking should be avoided, or at least incorporated only occasionally, to fall in line with the nutritional guidelines.

No repeats in foods

Commodities should not be repeated in the same menu. For example, serving steak and kidney pie for a main course followed by apple pie for dessert or serving tomato soup as a starter and having tomato *concassé* as a garnish for the main course is not good menu planning. It is very easy to fall into the trap of repeats especially when planning an à la carte menu. Sometimes repeats in foods on a menu cannot be helped but they should be avoided as much as possible.

Colour

The attractiveness of the food on the plate is very important to the customers' appreciation of a meal. So when planning a menu it is essential to try and visualize what the meal will look like on the plate – is it colourful, do the colours of food clash with each other, is it attractive? I once had a meal which tasted very good as long as you ate with your eyes shut! The meal was served on a white plate and consisted of breast of chicken with a white wine sauce, new potatoes which had been peeled, cauliflower, and peeled courgettes. The overall effect was white and very bland although the food was beautifully cooked. To improve the meal all that was needed was the inclusion of more colourful vegetables. However, serving colours that clash, such as red cabbage with carrots and tomatoes, will be equally off-putting.

Texture

Varying textures of food is also important. Using soft foods alongside crisp foods with sauces and drier foods will give a variety of 'bite' to the menu. Again the caterer needs to try to get the 'feel' of the meal on the plate at the initial stages of menu planning.

Nutritional balance

This area is often overlooked by caterers but it is hoped that this book has perhaps put the record straight! Nutritional balance is not just for hospital catering or residential homes, it is important for every customer eating at any type of catering establishment. The customer should be able to choose or be given a good nutritionally balanced meal. However, different groups in the community have different nutritional needs and we shall look at these shortly.

Nutritional guidelines

It would be foolish to ignore the advice of experts with regard to the relationship between diet and our health. In fact caterers could play an important role in encouraging their customers towards a healthier diet by applying the concepts of healthy eating in the menu. Looking at the types of food used and the cooking methods involved when planning menus would help to achieve this goal.

Special needs

Including dishes which will be suitable for people following certain types of diet is another important factor in menu planning. Catering for vegetarians, vegans, 'ethnic' and weight reduction diets will help customer choice and even enhance the reputation of the catering establishment.

Time

Knowing the times of service is important. Does the menu have to cover breakfast, lunch and dinner or just some of these? Do snack foods have to be considered? Another factor is the length of time available to prepare and cook the dishes – a dish which will take several hours to prepare and cook is not suitable on a menu if only one hour can be allocated.

These 15 points add up to form the most relevant criteria for menu planning. You may be able to add to the list. Each item is worth considering before attempting to plan a menu.

Catering for different nutritional needs

Before we look at different types of catering establishment and their specific needs in menu planning, let us look in detail at the **nutritional needs** of various groups within the community. We started off in this book looking at the influences that affect our choice of food. We have also highlighted our differences in height, age, body shape, occupation and lifestyle; at certain times in our lives we have particular nutritional needs and we shall now explore these further.

Children

Infants and young children

Up to the age of six months a baby relies solely on milk to provide all the nutrients its body requires. Breast milk can provide all these needs, or there are also a number of proprietary milks available. These milks should be supplemented with drinks of cooled boiled water or diluted fruit juice to cleanse the palate and, in the case of the juice, to provide extra vitamin C. Remember that babies, although rapidly growing, are not expending much physical energy and so their energy needs will be relatively low; if they eat too much, weight gain can be too rapid. Another important point about babies is that when they are born the digestive system has never been used and it takes some months for it to get into full gear. To start with, not all the enzymes that are part of an adult's digestion are produced, so giving 'meat and two veg' to a young baby is doing far more harm than good!

Semi-solid food is typically introduced from six months, and as teeth start to appear a more mixed food diet can be introduced, using different textures and tastes. By the time a baby is a year old the digestive system will be in full working order and the taste buds are fully developed. But milk will still play an important role in the diet, producing a good basic supply of nutrients for the body to rely on. Skimmed milk should not be given to children under five years of age as their main source of milk. Semi-skimmed or whole milk will help provide the essential fatty acids their bodies require.

Schoolchildren

Nutritional requirements for children at this stage are high in relation to body size. The energy requirements and the body's needs for calcium, protein and iron are higher than for adults. Children go through a growth spurt around seven to nine years of age, so nutritional requirements are high at this time. Children will also be more active and many have larger appetites than adults, not necessarily eating vast quantities of food at a time but little and very often! This age often determines future eating habits, and likes and dislikes in food are very prominent. It is important to try to encourage as many different foods in the diet as possible to give the body a chance to obtain a wide variety of nutrients. However, the very distinct likes and dislikes that children have can make this a frustrating age for the caterer.

Adolescents

Nutritional needs are in many respects higher during this time than for any other group. Growth spurts and puberty require a good nutritional intake, including carbohydrates, fats, and a good supply of protein, vitamins and minerals. However, it is also a time of high emotional changes which can influence the frequency of eating and the type of foods chosen. Providing a good varied selection of foods should go a long way in fulfilling nutritional needs during this time.

Pregnancy and lactation

As would be expected, the nutritional needs of this group are high. During pregnancy, a woman's body has to adapt to form a completely new human being and must supply all the nutritional needs of the unborn child. The old wives' tale of eating for two does not apply, but good supplies of protein, vitamins and minerals are very important, with sufficient energy foods to allow for growth but not excessive weight gain on the part of the mother-to-be.

Similarly, during lactation (breast feeding) there is also a strong demand for a good supply of all the nutrients. During this time, the mother must supply all the nutrients the baby needs to grow and the diet should reflect this. So sensitive is the body's mechanism that some foods eaten by the mother can affect the baby and cause colic. High-acid foods such as rhubarb and citrus fruits as well as alcohol can change the breast milk, causing upset to the baby.

The elderly

The ageing process causes the body to slow down, and physical activity diminishes, as does the need for energy-rich foods, although these are important to help maintain the body temperature. Elderly people can be prone to hypothermia (low body temperature), particularly those who are poor or who live alone, and energy foods will help to counteract this. The nutritional requirements needed to maintain the body in good health are high for this age group. The appetite tends to diminish, so small frequent meals are required to provide adequate levels of protein, energy foods, vitamins and minerals (particularly iron and calcium). High levels of fat foods could cause weight problems for some but carbohydrate should be included, particularly dietary fibre. This is important to aid the digestive system, which can become sluggish.

We have highlighted the nutritional needs of particular groups, taken into account any special dietary needs (see Chapter 9), discussed what is meant by nutritional guidelines and looked at the general criteria for menu planning. We can now apply this knowledge to the practicalities involved in running different catering establishments. These can be divided into two major areas, institutional catering and commercial catering.

Institutional catering

This area of catering covers establishments which have a strict budget and tend to cater for the needs of customers within an organization. This may mean catering for a customer's complete dietary needs or it may mean providing just one meal a day.

School meals

For many parts of Britain this area of catering has diminished since the change in the Education Act (1980). However, many county councils still provide a wide range of meals for both primary and secondary schools.

Up to school age, the family is the major influence on a child's eating habits. At school, the influence changes to encompass school friends of the same age, teachers, television and advertisements. Children become more independent about their likes and dislikes in food. On the whole, children are fairly 'finicky' eaters and are also erratic, eating well for one meal and then poorly at others. They are also very conservative in their likes and dislikes and will quite happily eat the same lunch (such as beefburger and chips or just chips on their own) every day.

For teenagers, emotional problems can influence their eating habits and cause loss of appetite. Environmental issues are also particularly important to this age group and alternative forms of eating, such as vegetarianism, can become popular.

These factors should be considered when planning a menu. All too often the tendency is to provide the children with foods that are considered to be popular, regardless of whether they are nutritionally sound. These foods are known as fast foods (junk foods by some people). A typical meal using such foods might be sausages/beefburgers, baked beans and chips followed by cakes of various descriptions. This is not good menu planning; a more varied choice is required. At this age it is very important to 'sow the seeds' for later life on aspects of diet and health and to introduce a menu which cuts down fats, sugars and salt and increases fibre intake. This can be achieved by providing interesting and popular items such as jacket potatoes with various fillings, chicken and fish dishes, or trying different forms of cuisine such as a Mexican week or Italian dishes. Perhaps a bit gimmicky, but it could prove fun as well as provide a more healthy variety of foods. Some children rely on the school meal as the main meal of the day, whereas for others it is merely a snack to see them through to their main meal at home in the evening. The caterer should take this into account and provide the equivalent to a packed lunch, offering filled rolls, sandwiches or baguettes, using wholemeal bread as well as white bread. Many parents would welcome a move like this which would save them the time involved in preparing a packed lunch for their child.

Many school meals services offer a choice of dishes in either a cafeteria or a family-type system. Although a choice is important to help cater for all needs, a large array of foods can be rather daunting to a child or young teenager. The majority of children do not have a say in what they eat at home; it is more likely that the choice will be made for them by adults. To suddenly be faced with having to make a choice for a school lunch may prove very difficult. I once watched an 11-year-old girl eat her way through seven cakes she had lined up in front of her in a school canteen.

There was no main course in sight and she had just chosen the cakes. When asked 'Why seven cakes and no first course?', she pointed out that she did not like the look of the main courses, but the cakes looked so good she was unable to choose just one so had one of each! Choice is important but a limited choice would be wiser, and giving the children some form of training in making an informed choice, either in the form of colour coding or as a points system would be of help. It is important to allow for some kind of nutritional compensation while planning the menu to cover loss of vitamins and minerals during preparation, cooking and service.

Boarding schools and residential homes for children

The same points as noted above for school meals also apply to this group. However, the added dimension is that *all* the dietary needs of the children have to be catered for. Careful consideration should therefore be given to the nutritional value of the meals. Variety in foods is important to help provide a wide range of all the nutrients and also to maintain interest. This perhaps goes against the idea that children are conservative in their tastes, but nevertheless it is an area which should be emphasized. Presentation, colour and texture are very significant in encouraging children to be more adventurous about their choice of food. Offering meals which include the nutritional guidelines is also very important as this can start to influence eating habits for the future. This can be achieved, even on a tight budget, by including porridge, Weetabix, shredded wheat and wholemeal bread on the menu for breakfast to increase fibre content, by looking at how different cooking methods can reduce fat intake, and by introducing more chicken and fish dishes, to give just some examples. Careful consideration of losses due to preparation and cooking are very important for this group as the pupils rely solely on the food provided for their dietary needs.

Universities and colleges of further/higher education

This area of institutional catering is also concerned with all aspects of the students' dietary needs. Thus the concepts of a nutritionally balanced diet and the inclusion of nutritional guidelines into the menu are of prime importance and have unfortunately too often been overlooked. Many catering establishments in this category have to cater for a number of ethnic diets for overseas students and have to take into account dietary laws and religious festivals.

Most students will at this stage have a different concept of food from their schooldays. They demand a good choice in dishes, reasonably large portions and value for money! Involving students by having a 'suggestions box' or a students' representative will help to ensure co-operation all round. Colour and presentation of food are also important factors.

Many colleges also cater for academic staff and for conferences during the vacations. This can necessitate a variety in the service and meals provided. But the main criterion for menu planning stays the same: the importance of supplying the dietary needs of all customers. A captive audience like students, staff or delegates to a conference brings an added dimension to the concept of nutritional needs.

Industrial canteens

Many firms provide catering facilities for their staff. Some employ their own catering staff, while others rely on contract caterers. However, there are also a growing number of employers who now only supply vending machines for snacks and drinks for their employees – a sad development.

This type of catering aims to provide a midday meal and possibly snacks for the workforce of an industrial firm. The catering budget is sometimes subsidized by the firm, enabling the caterer to provide very reasonable meals to all the staff. Some firms also rely on the caterer to provide meals for visiting clients, which can add variety to the type of service provided.

As only one meal of the day is offered, the need for catering for all the customers' nutritional needs does not apply. But it is important that the menu is such that customers can make a good nutritional choice and can choose from snacks, salads and a two- or three-course meal. Incorporating dishes which reflect the nutritional guidelines is important in enabling customers to make wise choices. This should apply to conference-type meals, business lunches and other functions. Some caterers in industrial canteens in England and Wales have got involved with the Health Education Authority's 'Look after Your Heart Campaign' to help prevent heart disease. This has meant changing menus and incorporating more fibre foods and less fat, sugar and salt. Many of these campaigns have been very successful.

Some firms require their staff to do shift work, so, although still only offering one meal per customer, the caterer has to provide a round-the-clock service. More are turning to cook-chill or cook-freeze with microwave cookers for re-heating, to overcome the problem of staffing a kitchen 24 hours a day, 7 days a week. Some foods do not lend themselves to the cook-freeze method as their keeping qualities are not high. Cook-chill appears to be a more popular option and either this can be incorporated in the existing day menu, or a separate menu can be developed. Strict hygiene safeguards must be observed with cook-freeze and cook-chill, but the nutritional value of the meals should be no different to that of normal dishes.

Hospitals

This area of industrial catering is probably the largest and the most difficult to organize and run. The majority of hospitals are big, serving a wide population with a large number of beds and an even larger number of staff. So the hospital caterer is faced with providing not only all the meals for the patients, but also those for a large number of resident and non-resident staff. There is the added factor that most of the patients are not in hospital for a holiday but are ill and food may not be appetizing for them – the caterer must try and overcome this problem. This area of catering probably comes in for the most criticism from both inside and outside the Health Service, but most of the critics have little idea of the problems facing the caterer in hospitals. These problems need to be highlighted to enable us to make recommendations with regard to menu planning.

Let us look at the patients first. In all general hospitals the types of illness suffered by the patients will be very diverse – some will have broken bones while others will have internal ailments. The difference in appetite and need for food will vary enormously. For example, an orthopaedic ward will require meals which are substantial as the majority of the patients will have good appetites. The other end of the spectrum is the intensive care ward, where patients may not be eating at all, or a ward of patients who need nourishing food to help restore their health but have little desire to eat. All these differences must be catered for on a menu. These hospitals also have a special diet area in the kitchen which will supply food for certain patients who require a modification in normal eating as part of the treatment for their condition. A hospital dietitian will assist a caterer in this area, but many of these diets have to be catered for off the menu. Eating is a very important part of the hospital day, but it must be fitted around a lot of other activities such as doctors' ward rounds and treatments. It is not unusual for hospital food trolleys to sit on a ward long after a mealtime because of a delay of some kind. This practice should not be allowed as food plays a major part in *all* patients' treatment, providing valuable nutrients to help the healing process. The longer the food is left about before eating, the more it will deteriorate and the greater the loss of nutrients will be. The patient population of a general hospital is very fluid, with some patients in for a few days, some for a week and others for longer. Keeping up with numbers and tracking down special needs can be a major problem for the caterer, and communications are not always good between wards and kitchen. Finally, the budget for food is low. Unfortunately, the catering budget comes way down the pecking order in terms of money needs in a busy hospital. Thus a caterer has to cope with providing three meals a day on a very limited budget.

How can menu planning overcome these problems? Working within a strict budget is never easy but many district and regional health authorities have negotiated contracts with wholesalers for a number of hospital catering departments. These contracts, which are reviewed every year, help to keep costs under control by allowing food to be bought in bulk. This is possible because the majority of menus produced are on a cycle system – sometimes monthly, six-weekly or even eight-weekly.

Producing a choice in the menu for each meal will help to provide for special diets as well as cater for the needs of individual appetites: providing a light meal alongside more substantial dishes will help. Traditionally we were thought to require three cooked meals a day. In fact, few people either have or need as much but it has taken institutional catering a long time to realize this. Hospitals used to produce a cooked breakfast, lunch and dinner despite the fact that half the patients probably did not have the appetite for them! Today, more offer a choice of a light breakfast as well as a cooked one, with a cooked lunch and a lighter supper. This seems sound practice.

The nutritional balance of the menu is of great importance for this type of catering. The food that is offered to every patient is essential in aiding the healing process. The menu should provide a good protein content, as well as vitamins and minerals to help the healing and repair process, and energy foods to give the body a chance to recover. Care needs to be taken in preparing and cooking the food to ensure minimal nutritional loss; in this respect it is particularly important to think about the holding and serving of foods. Hospitals, on the whole, are sprawling buildings with food having to travel in trolleys for some distance from the kitchen to the wards. The menu must take into account the travelling problems – some dishes, such as a cheese soufflé or a milk shake, do not travel! Some foods need to be served straight away and quickly deteriorate if over-cooked. Scrambled egg is a classic example and one which frequently appears on a menu as it is a relatively light dish. Unfortunately it turns solid and unappetizing with time.

Nutritional guidelines should be incorporated into the choice of meals and every encouragement given to the patients to follow such advice. If a hospital cannot implement this advice, who can! Colour, texture and presentation of dishes must be thought of during the planning stage as this is an important way to tempt dwindling appetites. Many catering departments have a plated meals system, which means the food is plated in

the kitchen and taken to the patient in special containers in trolleys. This helps the catering staff have more control over the presentation of the meals.

We have concentrated here on general hospital catering, but the same criteria apply to other types of hospital – maternity, geriatric, psychiatric, children's and hospices. Their basic needs – and problems – are the same.

Alongside the patients' meals go the staff meals, and many caterers produce a separate menu for staff requirements. This is to help the staff, who have seen the patients have their meals, enjoy a different type of dish. Staff meals are usually served on a cafeteria system, with staff paying directly for their meals. Resident staff rely on the catering service for all their dietary needs and the menu must reflect this in terms of both nutritional balance and nutritional guidelines.

Small hospital units are tending to rely on cook-chill foods to provide the catering service, and a number of firms are involved with this. Many private hospitals employ contract caterers to service their needs. Either way the criteria for catering for the hospital service are the same.

Residential homes for the elderly

Most of these homes are run by local authorities, although in the present political climate many of them are being closed to make way for privately run homes. This area of catering has always been poorly funded with very limited resources for food and staffing costs. The residents of these homes are not ill, just ageing both physically and mentally. Food and the meals provided are often for many of the residents the highlight of the day.

When planning menus a few important points are worth emphasizing. It could be argued that those who have reached the age of 75 are entitled to eat whatever they want without worrying about nutritional content and nutritional guidelines! There is certainly quite a bit of truth in this; however, the life people lead should be the fullest possible and the quality of life high. To help achieve this it is important to emphasize the nutritional needs, for this is another area of catering where all the dietary needs of the individual must be met. Elderly people in residential homes tend to be less active physically, and so their need for energy decreases. Central heating will help prevent hypothermia, so the need for high-energy foods is much less, and if not reduced could result in weight gain. Protein foods should include a good supply of high biological value proteins, which are easy to digest; hard-boiled eggs and cheese are not easy foods to digest. Nutrients released during digestion may not be so easily absorbed with increasing age, and so the diet must contain an increased amount of vitamins and minerals to compensate for this, along with a good supply of dietary fibre to assist the digestive system. Calcium, iron and vitamin C and D foods should be emphasized on the menu. Varying the foods will also help towards achieving a balanced diet.

Lack of teeth or badly fitting dentures can make eating very difficult for residents. It is not unknown for people to take out their teeth to eat their meals! It is important to have soft foods on the menu – stews, casseroles, cottage pie are just a few examples – and the food does not have to be puréed. Giving a 'soft' choice on the menu will help to cater for all needs. The senses of smell and taste also decline with age and as these are important in our appreciation of food this may adversely affect an individual's food intake. A chef will come to know his/her residents and be able to judge the required seasoning.

Ageing impairs the secretion of saliva, stomach acids and other digestive juices and some people find digesting food difficult. Having a large evening meal will cause great discomfort to many elderly people, so the main meal of the day should be at midday with a light supper or high tea in the evening. Some foods will no longer be acceptable for many residents as they may cause indigestion. Acid foods such as citrus fruits and cheese are common culprits. Most of the residents will have reduced appetites so small meals often is recommended.

Lack of co-ordination and a loss of muscle activity following a stroke or as the result of arthritis can affect people's capacity to eat. The effort involved in cutting meat or vegetables and getting the food from the plate to the mouth can prove an enormous task for those with such afflictions. Again, including soft foods and ready peeled fruits on the menu, as well as providing specially adapted knives, forks and spoons, will ease their distress.

Colour and presentation of meals is of prime importance to tempt the palate, so the meals must look attractive as well as taste good. Consideration as to what the food will look like on the plate is essential in the planning stage. A choice of foods on the menu will help cater for likes and dislikes as well as giving a light alternative. The elderly have always been considered to be very traditional in their eating habits, eating what is termed traditional British fare. Introducing curries, spicy food, pasta and other ethnic dishes is considered taboo. However, this is changing as the elderly of today and tomorrow are becoming more familiar with different types of dishes and eating styles. Perhaps today we should consider more traditional foods but in a decade's time a more varied worldwide selection of dishes could be included!

Commercial catering

This area of catering has snowballed since the mid-1970s and now forms a major part of the leisure industry. 'Eating out' has become a very important social activity for an increasing number of people and more and more food outlets have developed to meet these needs. Commercial catering is big business, with an increasing turnover in income, profits and staff. Hotels, restaurants, pubs, clubs and fast-food outlets are all included in this section.

Hotels

The tourist trade and businessmen/women have been mainly responsible for the increase in the number of hotels and guest-houses. For a hotel the cuisine offered can be of prime importance in attracting its clientele. Many hotels diversify to offer different forms of cuisine, for example they might have a carvery, a salad bar for quick meals, and a restaurant with full silver service and à la carte menu. Obviously what is offered will depend on the size of the hotel and also its location. Many small hotels offer half board with bed and breakfast and an evening meal, with the latter open to non-residents. For larger hotels non-residential customers can make up half the trade and a good restaurant can attract business. Many of these hotels offer conference facilities and also cater for banquets, wedding receptions and parties. So the catering requirements can be quite varied. Food costs are usually higher in this form of catering than in those previously discussed, but budgets are still important to ensure the right level of profit. The manager of a hotel will be only too aware of the limitations that money will put on the kind of food offered.

It has been argued that the nutritional aspects of menu planning and the nutritional guidelines apply only to institutional catering and especially hospitals, not to this sector. I hope I have helped to dispel this myth by showing why all sides of the catering industry should offer a nutritionally balanced diet to their customers. There are times when customers require a hotel to meet all their dietary needs, such as when they stay there for several days or weeks. It is then that the caterer needs to provide for all the nutritional requirements. It is also important to incorporate the nutritional guidelines into menus so that customers can make informed choices. This does not mean that the whole menu should reflect 'healthy eating', but that there should be enough dishes which incorporate the guidelines for customers to choose from if they wish. The increasing interest in vegetarianism should encourage the caterer to offer such a choice on a menu. It may also be necessary to cater for 'ethnic' diets as well as some special diets.

Colour, texture and presentation are very important to attract and stimulate the palate, and these can also enhance the reputation of the hotel's restaurant. Visualizing the food on the plate is important in the planning stage. This applies especially to the choice of vegetables, which have to fit in with all dishes from carvery ones to an à la carte menu. Vegetable preparation can result in large losses in vitamin C (as we have seen in Chapter 5), but this could be overcome by including a green vegetable of high vitamin C content as one of the choices as well as including other foods on the menu to compensate for this loss.

Many hotels will cook to order although the preparation may have taken place hours before. The organization of the kitchen is very important in helping to maintain the nutritional value of the food as well as its colour and quality.

Restaurants

Much of the advice given for hotels applies also to this area of catering. The main difference is that the majority of restaurants do not offer such a wide variety of food service as a large hotel. Many restaurants specialize in a certain type of cooking, for example British, Chinese, Mexican, Greek, Indian or vegetarian food.

Menus should reflect value for money as well as expertise in specialist dishes to help promote the business. Once a reputation is made for both food and service, this has to be maintained by continual high standards. It is a hard life for a good restaurateur! The majority of restaurants offer both a lunch and dinner service and the menu will be different for each. The caterer must be aware of the needs of the customers and these should be reflected in the menu. Should the lunch be a set menu with a fast service if he/she is catering for office staff? Should there be an alternative choice to attract businessmen/women who will entertain clients and require a more relaxed atmosphere? These points need to be considered when planning the menu.

A restaurant is catering for only a small part of a person's daily nutritional intake and the customers may not be regulars. Many people eat out in a restaurant as a treat or on a special occasion and their nutritional needs are far from their minds! Perhaps the emphasis on nutrition need not be so great in this sector but it should still be considered. Producing a nutritionally balanced meal, and one which avoids the loss of nutrients which can occur during preparation and cooking, should be second nature to a chef. Planning a menu, whether it is a set menu or à la carte, should always reflect nutritional considerations.

Incorporating the nutritional guidelines of reducing the fat, sugar and salt content of meals and increasing dietary fibre is important. As with hotels, this does not mean that the whole menu needs to show these considerations, but certainly dishes should be incorporated into the menu which reflect them. There are some excellent dishes that would enhance any menu which are not only attractive, appetizing, filling and taste good but also conform to nutritional guidelines. It is sad that the myth has arisen that eating in this way is boring and unimaginative and a good and enjoyable meal must be laced with butter and cream! Many customers are very concerned about their health and would welcome the concern a restaurateur or chef would show by including such dishes and taking care over cooking methods.

Pubs and clubs

In the past decade more of this sector has expanded into the catering business. Clubs, whether private clubs, golf clubs or clubs for other leisure pursuits, have always offered catering facilities to their members but this has increased in recent years. With the advent of drink-drive laws, more public houses are providing bar snacks or more substantial meals for their customers as a way of increasing business.

Knowing the customer is a basic criterion in planning the menu. For clubs this may not prove difficult as the membership will provide this information. It is not so easy for the landlord. However, the locality of the pub will help. Developing a good quality bar snack or restaurant service as well as good bar service can attract customers from afar as a reputation spreads. Regularly changing the menu or offering speciality dishes of the day can keep the interest of the clientele. There is nothing worse than seeing the same old menu week after week! Colour, texture, presentation and quality of meals are important points to remember in planning the menu. Providing a wide variety of dishes to cater for all tastes will also help.

If the customers are regular eaters in either a pub or a club they should be able to choose a nutritionally balanced diet and, as with restaurants, enough choices should be incorporated to reflect the nutritional guidelines. So many catering establishments in this category will serve chips with everything without considering alternatives. The caterer can influence people's eating habits and develop an enjoyable eating experience which will also take care of health.

Fast-food outlets

This sector of catering has grown tremendously over the past ten years, not only in Britain but also in other parts of the world. The increase in leisure time and the development of a more affluent society has meant more people eating out and a greater demand for quick, ready-prepared meals or snacks. These meals are eaten at the catering outlet, in the street, in the car or at home!

The types of establishments in this category vary enormously and many specialize in certain types of snack food. Some examples are:

coffee bars – offering drinks, sandwiches, cakes and pastries
fish and chip bars
pizza parlours and kebab bars
beefburger/chicken bars
hot-dog stands
sandwich bars and jacket potato bars
tea rooms – specializing in afternoon tea
Chinese/Indian take-aways
transport cafés

It is very easy to condemn some of these outlets as serving junk food which pays little attention to nutritional requirements. True, the emphasis for some is on a fast turnover of food, much of which is bought in ready prepared, requiring the minimum of cooking and the least amount of skill. But this is an over-simplification of the issue. The majority of fast-food outlets actually supply a good product at a reasonable price and many staff take great pride in their work, but unfortunately nutritional issues are not always considered.

As far as menu planning is concerned, the speciality will dictate the type of menu offered to the customer, and the criteria discussed at the beginning of this chapter apply just as much to this group of catering outlets as to others we have looked at. For example, a fish and chip bar often includes sausages, pies and chicken on the menu along with mushy peas, but the main item on the menu is fish and chips. The menu could include many different types of fish, not just cod, haddock or plaice. This is becoming more common as we gradually deplete the fish stocks in the sea. However, there is no way that a fish and chip meal can be considered nutritionally balanced or can comply with the nutritional guidelines. The fish and chips could be fried in a pure vegetable oil, the fish could be battered using wholemeal flour rather than white, but this would make little difference to the overall effect. There are some meals which cannot be changed to comply nutritionally and this is one. It remains for individual customers to decide how often this type of meal should appear in their diet.

Other outlets could and do comply with the nutritional guidelines – some coffee bars, sandwich bars and tea rooms offer wholemeal bread as well as white for sandwiches and filled rolls. Many use a pure vegetable margarine as well as butter and a number offer skimmed or semi-skimmed milk for drinks. But much more could be done to help the health of the nation. For example, much of the snack food in transport cafés and snack bars could be grilled or poached rather than fried, and other types of potato offered as well as chips. In pasta parlours wholemeal pasta could be offered as well as white pasta; brown rice could be served in Chinese/Indian take-aways, and wholemeal buns served with grilled beefburger and salad in a beefburger bar. This would offer the customer a choice of a meal with a higher fibre content. Providing low-fat fillings for sandwiches and filled rolls, cutting down on fried foods and chips, offering low-fat fillings for jacket potatoes, and providing alternatives to cream cakes and gâteaux, will all go some way towards reducing the fat content of meals. Making such small changes means that there should be no extra cost to the customer.

These fast-food outlets provide a useful service to the public and are very popular. With a little thought and some changes, they could provide an even better service by offering a choice which will incorporate the nutritional guidelines and help to educate customers in a healthier way of eating. It could also boost sales and profits as people come to realize that eating out is fun and also healthy!

We have concentrated on a number of catering establishments in this chapter, looking at important points which should be taken into consideration when planning menus for the different services they provide. It is hoped that this information will prove of use to the chef/caterer. The emphasis has been on the nutritional balance of the menu and on the inclusion of nutritional guidelines as this is an area which sadly is so often overlooked. Appendix I lists the main nutrients, giving good food sources which should assist in helping to plan the nutritional aspects of the menu, and Appendices II and III provide a checklist to see if this goal has been achieved! But no matter how balanced in nutrients the menu, or how much it complies with all the basic criteria for good menu planning, it is the preparation, cooking and serving of the food which holds the secret to success. This is down to the chef and his/her staff. The nutritional value of the end product is dependent on good kitchen practices and I hope this book has gone some way towards explaining these in more detail.

Checksheet

Try to answer the following questions.

1. List ten points to be taken into consideration when menu planning.

a.	*f.*
b.	*g.*
c.	*h.*
d.	*i.*
e.	*j.*

2. The digestive system is in full working order in a new-born baby. True or false.

3. Children have a growth spurt between the ages of:
   a. 5–6 years   *b.* 6–8 years   *c.* 7–9 years   *d.* 10–12 years.

4. List three nutrients which should be part of the diet of elderly people.
   a.   *b.*   *c.*

5. Name the two major areas of catering.
   a.   *b.*

6. Give three examples of catering establishments within each area named in Question 5.

a.   a.

b.   b.

c.   c.

7. School meals should meet all the child's nutritional needs. True or false.

8. List two foods which could increase the dietary fibre content of breakfast at a boarding school.

a.   b.

9. Name three problems a hospital caterer has to overcome when planning menus for a general hospital.

a.

b.

c.

10. Give three considerations which are important in the planning of meals for the elderly in a residential home.

a.

b.

c.

11. Suggest one way a caterer could compensate for the loss of vitamin C during preparation of vegetables.

12. Name four examples of fast-food outlets.

a.   c.

b.   d.

Now turn to the text to check you answers.

Further study

Complete the following tasks.

1. Collect a number of menus from a variety of different catering establishments. Compare the menus by using the criteria for menu planning described in the text.

2. Visit a school, hospital or residential home for the elderly. Write a report on the catering facilities offered and produce a week's menu of your own. Remember to follow the criteria suggested.

3. Visit the pubs in your locality to find out the type of meals on offer. Write a report that compares the menus you have collected and make recommendations on how they can be improved.

Good food sources of the nutrients

The following lists indicate good food sources of all the different nutrients. Their purpose is to help the chef/caterer identify foods which will supply a high proportion of a particular nutrient. Food tables (see p. 157) will supply the amount in grams of each of the nutrients contained in a particular quantity of food. It is important to note that as the majority of our food contains a mixture of different nutrients, so some foods will appear in several of the lists.

Note: *Denotes a very good food source.

Protein

High biological value proteins

*All cuts of meat and offal – beef, lamb and pork, rabbit, venison
*All poultry – chicken, turkey, duck, goose, guinea fowl
*All fish – oily and white fish
*Milk – whole, semi-skimmed, skimmed, powdered or liquid
*Cheese – all types
*Eggs – fresh, dried or pasteurized
*Soya beans – soya bean flour, textured vegetable protein

Low biological value proteins

*Cereals – rice, rye, wheat, barley
*Cereal products – bread, breakfast cereals, biscuits, pasta, all products made with flour (white or wholemeal)
*Nuts and seeds – all types
Potatoes
*Pulses – beans, peas, lentils

Carbohydrates

Sugars

*Granulated sugar
*Demerara sugar
*Light/dark brown sugar
*Icing/castor sugar
*Sweets – all types
*Chocolate/chocolates
*Jam and marmalade
*Honey, syrup, treacle

*Iced cakes
All cakes and sweet biscuits
*Fizzy drinks and fruit squashes
Fruit canned in syrup
Steamed puddings and desserts
Milk
Fresh and *dried fruit
*Sweet wines/sherries

Starch

*Cereals – rice, wheat, barley, rye	*Pasta
*Bread – all types	Roux-based sauces
*Breakfast cereals – all types	*Cakes, pastry/pastries
Cornflour	*Biscuits – sweet/savoury
*Flour – white and wholemeal	*Root vegetables – potatoes

Dietary fibre

*All vegetables – fresh, frozen, canned or dried – particularly unpeeled
*All fruit – fresh, frozen, canned or dried – particularly unpeeled
*Brown rice
*Wholegrain breakfast cereals – Weetabix, Shredded Wheat, puffed wheat, Sugar Puffs, porridge oats, oat cereal, Shreddies, wheat flakes
*Bran breakfast cereals – Allbran, Bran Buds, Branflakes, Fruit and Fibre
*Wholemeal bread/rolls
*Granary bread/rolls
*Wholemeal pasta
*Wholemeal flour
*Biscuits made with wholemeal flour or rye flour – ryvita, vita-wheat, digestives, bran biscuits
Nuts – all types
Seeds – sunflower seeds
Pulses – peas, beans, lentils

Fats

Animal fats

*Butter
*Dripping
*Lard
*Suet
*Cream – single, half-fat, whipping, double, clotted
*Milk – whole
*Cheese – all types except cottage cheese
*Fatty meat – beef, lamb, pork
*Full-fat yogurts and fromage frais
*Sausages, cooked meats

Vegetable fats

*Corn oil
*Sunflower oil
*Safflower oil
*Soya bean oil
*Groundnut oil
*Rapeseed oil
*Olive oil
*Blended vegetable oil
*Sunflower margarine
*Corn oil margarine
*Soya bean margarine
*Block margarines

*Pastry
Cakes – made with fat
*Shortbread
Biscuits – sweet
*Chocolate/chocolates
*Chocolate snack bars
*Fried foods – chips

Vitamins

Fat soluble vitamins

Vitamin A

*Butter
*Margarine
*Cream
*Cheese
Milk
*Egg yolks
Pastry/cakes made with
margarine/butter
Added to some breakfast cereals

*Liver
Kidney
*Liver sausage
*Fatty fish – tuna, mackerel, herrings,
kippers, pilchards, sardines, trout,
salmon
*Low-fat spreads

Carotene (precursor of vitamin A)

All green vegetables
*Tomatoes
*Tomato purée
Tomato sauce
*Red/green peppers
Sweet potatoes
*Watercress
*Carrots
*Sweetcorn
*Fruit juice – orange, grapefruit

*Apricots
Apples
Bananas
Blackberries
Cherries
Blackcurrants
Figs
Damsons
Gooseberries
*Mangoes
*Peaches
*Nectarines
Plums
*Prunes
Raspberries
Strawberries
*Tangerines
Oranges

Vitamin D

Milk
Cream
*Cheese – all types
*Egg yolks
*Fatty fish – herring, kippers, mackerel, pilchards, salmon, tuna, trout
Added to some breakfast cereals

*Butter
*Margarine
*Low-fat spreads
*Liver – liver sausage

Vitamin E

*Breakfast cereal
*Biscuits/cakes/pastry
*Butter
Cream
Cheese – all types
Yogurt
*Egg yolks
*Margarine
Suet
*Low-fat spreads

All meats
Offal
*All fish – fatty fish
Shellfish
All vegetables
All fruit
*Nuts
*Mayonnaise
*French dressings
Tomato purée
Tomato sauce

Water soluble vitamins

Vitamin B group
Thiamin (B1)

*Wheat flour – all types
Oatmeal
*Rice – brown
Pasta
*Bread/rolls
*Breakfast cereals
Biscuits – sweet/savoury
Cakes/pastry
Milk
Eggs
Chocolate
Cocoa powder

All meats
Offal
Meat products
Fatty fish
Shellfish
Fish fingers/cakes
All vegetables
*Pulses
All fruits
*Nuts
Marmite/Bovril

Riboflavin (B2)

*Wheat flour – all types
Oatmeal
Rice – brown
Pasta
Breakfast cereals
Biscuits – sweet/savoury
Cakes/pastry
*Milk
Cream
Cheese – all types
Yogurt
*Marmite/Bovril

*All meats
*Offal
Meat products
All fish
Shellfish
Fish fingers/cakes
All vegetables
All fruit
Nuts
Chocolate
Beer
*Tea/coffee/cocoa

Niacin (nicotenic acid)

*Wheat flour – all types
Pasta
*Bread
Breakfast cereals
Biscuits – sweet/savoury
Cakes/pastry
Milk – all types
Cheese – all types
*Eggs
All fruits – *dried fruits
Chocolate
Beer

*All meats/poultry
*Offal
*Meat products
*All fish
*Fish fingers/cakes
Shellfish
All vegetables
*Pulses, potatoes
*Mushrooms
*Nuts
Coffee

B6

*Wheat flour – all types
Pasta
*Bread
Breakfast cereals
Biscuits – sweet/savoury
Cakes/pastry
Milk – all types
Cheese – all types
*Eggs
Nuts

All meats/poultry
Offal
Meat products
All fish
Shellfish – *crab, *shrimps, *oysters
All vegetables – *potatoes
All fruit
Chocolate

B12

Milk – all types
Cream
Cheese
*Eggs
*Beef
*Lamb
Meat products

*Pork
*Turkey
*All offal – *liver
*Fish – white and fatty
*Cod's roe
Beer

Vitamin C

Milk – all types
*All vegetables
Ackee
Broccoli tops
Cabbage
Cauliflower
Leeks
Lettuce
*Mustard and cress
Okra
Spring onions
*Parsley
Peas
Runner beans
*Green peppers
New potatoes
Radishes
Spinach
Spring greens
Swede
*Tomatoes
Turnip tops
*Watercress

Cream – all types
*All fruit
Avocado pears
Bananas
Bilberries
*Blackcurrants
Redcurrants
Gooseberries
*Grapefruit
*Guavas
*Lemons
Loganberries
Lychees
*Mandarin oranges
*Mangoes
Melon – honeydew, canteloupe
Passion fruit
Paw paw
*Pineapple
Raspberries
Strawberries
Tangerines
*Oranges
*Fruit juices – grapefruit, orange and pineapple

Minerals

Sodium

Porridge oats
Bread/rolls
Breakfast cereals
Biscuits/cakes/pastries
*Milk
Butter
*Cheese
*Eggs
*Bacon/ham
All meats – *salted meat
*Meat products
*Salt – table, cooking, rock, sea

Offal
*Canned vegetables
*Salted peanuts
*Salted crisps
All fish
*Smoked fish
Shellfish
Treacle/syrup
Cocoa
Sauces/pickles
*Bovril/Marmite/Oxo

Potassium

Flour – all types
Soya flour
Breakfast cereals
Biscuits/cakes/pastry
Milk
Cheese
Eggs
All meats/poultry
Offal
Meat products
Curry powder

*All fish
*Shellfish
*All vegetables
*Pulses
All fruits – *dried
Nuts
Treacle/syrup
Chocolate
*Fruit juice
Bovril/Marmite

Calcium

*Flour – all types
Bread
Soya flour
Muesli
Biscuits/cakes/pastry
*Milk
*Cheese

Eggs
All fish/shellfish
Meat
Green vegetables
Nuts – *almonds
Chocolate
Cocoa

Iron

Flour – all types
Breakfast cereals
Eggs
*Beef
*Lamb
*Pork
*Grouse, pheasant, pigeon, hare
*Venison
Bovril/Marmite/Oxo

*Offal – liver, kidney
Meat products – *black pudding
Pulses
Nuts
Treacle
Chocolate
Cocoa
Curry powder
Raisins

Copper

Breakfast cereals
Eggs
Milk
Cheese
All meats
*Offal – *liver
Meat products
All fish
Shellfish

All vegetables
All fruit
Nuts
Preserves
Sweets – most types
Chocolates
Cocoa
Beers, wines
Sauces/pickles

Zinc

Wholemeal flour
Wholemeal bread/rolls
Wholegrain breakfast cereals
Crispbreads
Milk (cow's) – *evaporated/*condensed
*Cheese
*Eggs
*All meats/poultry
Sauces/pickles

*Offal
*Meat products
Fish – *fatty fish
Shellfish
All vegetables
All fruit
*Nuts
*Cocoa

Menu check for nutritional balance using food groups

Nutritional analysis of a menu

It is important to assess if the menu you are preparing is nutritionally balanced. This can be a highly complex procedure, but it is possible to analyse a menu using a very simple method involving the eight food groups:

1. Bread and cereal group
2. Meat and fish group
3. Milk and dairy group
4. Fruit and vegetable group
5. Non-dairy fats group
6. Preserve group
7. Confectionery group
8. Alcohol group

The first four groups are known as the **primary food groups** as they supply a good variety of nutrients (see Figure 7.1 and Table 7.2).

A well-balanced menu will:

*   include the primary food groups 1 to 4.
*   represent food groups 1 to 4 more times than groups 5 to 8.
*   represent food groups 1 to 4 in fairly equal proportions.

If the menu does not do this, the dishes can be changed by adding missing food groups, increasing the number of underrepresented food groups, or replacing a dish with an alternative which will give a better balance. This can mean a change in the method of cooking, changing the garnish, or adding more cereal to the meal.

Where there is an à la carte menu in operation the procedure can be repeated to check on other choices of meals.

To clarify this procedure two examples of menus have been analysed (see pp. 150, 151), but a detailed account of what the tables mean is only given for Example 1.

The starter is oxtail soup, with the main ingredients being meat (oxtail) and vegetables for flavour and stock. The latter is not represented by the food groups but the other two ingredients are, so a cross is placed beside the meat and fish group and also the fruit and vegetable group.

The main course is Grilled Crumbed Breast of Chicken with Mushroom Sauce. Here the main ingredients are chicken and breadcrumbs, so the meat and fish group and the bread and cereal group are represented with a cross beside each. Mushroom sauce has as its main ingredients mushrooms and flour, representing the fruit and vegetable and the bread and cereal groups.

There are three vegetables on the menu – carrots, courgettes and jacket potatoes – so three crosses are put beside the fruit and vegetable group.

The dessert is Apple and Blackberry Crumble and Custard – here the fruit and vegetable group is represented along with the bread and cereal group, non-dairy fats group (for the margarine) and the preserve group for the sugar. The milk and dairy group and bread and cereal group are present in the custard.

The sundries include a bread roll, butter, glass of wine and coffee with milk. So bread and cereal group, milk and dairy group and the alcohol group are all represented.

When the crosses are counted for the whole menu, it can be seen that the majority of the menu falls within the primary food groups, indicating that many of the nutrients will be available for the customer from this meal. The meat and fish group and the milk and dairy group offer similar nutrients, so when added together combine with the other primary groups to offer a reasonable balance of nutrients.

Now do an analysis of a menu of your choice by using the blank Nutritional Analysis of a Menu on p. 152 and following the procedure laid out below:

1. Write out the menu at the top of the table. If there is a choice of meals on the menu, choose as though you were going to eat the meal.

2. Collect all the recipes for the dishes which are part of the chosen meal.

3. Taking each individual dish, determine which food groups are represented by the *main* ingredients in the recipe. For example in the model analysis given on p. 150, Grilled Crumbed Breast of Chicken, breadcrumbs and chicken are the main ingredients – represented by the bread and cereal group and meat and fish group respectively.

4. Using the table supplied, tick or cross the main food groups present for each dish on the menu – starter, main course, vegetables, dessert, sundries (such as bread roll, glass of fruit juice or wine, coffee).

5. Total the number of times each food group is represented on the whole menu.

6. From this information it is now possible to determine if the menu is nutritionally balanced.

It is hoped that this method will prove of use to the busy caterer in determining if the meals on offer to the customer are balanced or not. It is important to emphasize that this method can only be used as a quick analysis of a menu and has its limitations in providing a detailed nutritional account.

A further drawback of this method is that it does not take into account the fat, sugar, salt or fibre content of the meals. Appendix III provides a further check on a menu to overcome this problem.

Example 1. **Nutritional analysis of a menu**

Menu

Oxtail soup – wholemeal roll and butter

Grilled crumbed breast of chicken with mushroom sauce
Carrots
Courgettes
Jacket potatoes
Glass of wine

Apple and blackberry crumble and custard

Coffee

Food group	Starter	Total	Main course	Total	Vegetables	Total	Dessert	Total	Sundries	Total	Total for menu
1. Bread and cereal			× ×	2			× ×	2	×	1	5
2. Meat and fish	×	1	×	1							2
3. Milk and dairy							×	1	× ×	2	3
4. Fruit and vegetable	×	1	×	1	× × ×	3	×	1			6
5. Non-dairy fats							×	1			1
6. Preserve							×	1			1
7. Confectionery											
8. Alcohol									×	1	1

Comments: The primary food groups are all represented. with only a small number of items coming from groups 5–8. This gives an indication that the meal will provide a good mix of nutrients.

Example 2. **Nutritional analysis of a menu**

Menu

Whitebait – white roll and butter

Chicken sauté chasseur
Glazed carrots
Dauphine potatoes

Glass of wine

Chocolate gâteau

Coffee – liqueur brandy

Food group	Starter	Total	Main course	Total	Vegetables	Total	Dessert	Total	Sundries	Total	Total for menu
1. Bread and cereal	×	1			×	1			×	1	2
2. Meat and fish	×	1	×	1							2
3. Milk and dairy					× ×	2			× ×	2	4
4. Fruit and vegetable			×	1	× ×	1					2
5. Non-dairy fats	×	1	×	1	× ×	2					4
6. Preserve											
7. Confectionery							×	1			1
8. Alcohol									× ×	2	2

Comments: Although the primary food groups are represented so are groups 5, 7 and 8. This would indicate that although the meal will provide nutrients to the body, it probably will not do so in the correct balance. Changes in the meal should be made to lower the content of group 5 and increase the primary groups.

Nutritional analysis of a menu

Menu

Food group	Total	Total	Total	Total	Total	Total for menu
Bread and cereal						
Meat and fish						
Milk and dairy						
Fruit and vegetables						
Non-dairy fats						
Preserves						
Confectionery						
Alcohol						

Menu check for healthy eating

Nutritional guidelines encourage us to lower the quantity of fat, sugar and salt in our diet and to increase the dietary-fibre content, especially from cereal products. It is important therefore that the caterer and chef is able to check the menu offered to the customer to see if it complies with the guidelines. The following lists give the foods which are high in fat, salt, sugar and dietary fibre.

Foods high in fat

All fried foods
Biscuits containing fat/oil
Butter
Cakes made with fat/oil
Cheese, except low-fat and cottage cheese
Chocolate
Chocolate biscuits and snack bars
Cooking fats – lard, dripping, vegetable fats
Cream – single, half, whipping, double, clotted
Crisps and corn snacks
Dairy ice cream
Egg yolks
Fatty meats – beef, lamb, pork, duck, goose
Foods canned in oil
Full-fat yogurts/fromage frais/quark
Full-fat milk, evaporated milk
Margarine and alternative spreads
Mayonnaise
Nuts
Pastry – shortcrust, rough puff, sweet paste, puff, suet
Peanut butter
Puddings – steamed and baked
Salad dressings – thousand island, seafood, garlic, French (vinaigrette)
Toffee, fudge, butterscotch
Vegetable oils

Foods high in salt

Bacon
Cooked sausage – e.g. salami
Ham
Salt – table, cooking, rock, sea
Salted crisps/snacks
Salt meat – e.g. salt beef
Salted peanuts
Sausages
Smoked fish – smoked haddock, cod and mackerel

Foods high in sugar

All types of sweets – boiled, jellied, fondants, fudge, toffee, butterscotch, mints
All puddings, cakes and desserts
Biscuits – sweet, iced, cream and chocolate
Chocolate/chocolates
Chocolate snack bars
Condensed milk
Fizzy drinks – lemonade, coke, mixer drinks
Fruit canned in syrup
Fruit squashes
Honey
Iced cakes
Jam, marmalade, syrup, treacle
Sugar – cane, castor, coffee crystals, demerara, icing, light/dark brown

Foods high in dietary fibre

All vegetables – fresh, frozen, canned and dried
All fruit – fresh, frozen, canned and dried
Biscuits – digestive, bran, Hovis, Ryvita, Vitawheat and all biscuits made with wholemeal or rye flour
Breakfast cereals – Weetabix, Shredded Wheat, puffed wheat, muesli, porridge oats, oat cereals, Shreddies, bran cereals (Allbran, Branflakes, Bran Buds, Fruit and Fibre)
Brown rice
Granary bread
Products made with wholemeal flour – pastry, sauces, cakes
Pulses – peas, beans, lentils, baked beans
Unpeeled vegetables – e.g. jacket potatoes
Unpeeled fruits – e.g. apples, pears
Wholemeal bread/rolls/pitta bread
Wholemeal flour
Wholemeal pasta

Using these lists and the table shown on p. 156, it is possible to determine if a menu is low in fat, sugar and salt, and high in fibre. The procedure is as follows:

1. The menu for analysis is written onto the table.

2. With the help of the lists of foods shown above, dishes are given a cross if they are high in fat, sugar, salt or dietary fibre.

3. The quantity of crosses for each column is added up.

4. The total for fat, sugar, salt should be under five, and for dietary fibre five or over.

The two menus analysed in Appendix II have been used as examples to show how the Healthy Eating Check works. As can be seen, one menu complies with the nutritional guidelines, whereas the second example does not. It should be pointed out that wholemeal flour was used for breadcrumbs and in the crumble dessert in

Healthy eating check using Appendix II, Example 1

Menu	Fat	Sugar	Salt	Dietary fibre
Oxtail soup				
Wholemeal roll				×
Butter	×			
Grilled crumbed breast of chicken with mushroom sauce	×		×	
Carrots			×	×
Courgettes			×	×
Jacket potato with yogurt dressing				×
Apple and blackberry crumble	×	×		×
Custard (skimmed milk)		×		
Coffee – milk (semi-skimmed)				
Total	3	2	3	5

Comments: The meal is low in fat, sugar and salt and relatively high in dietary fibre.

Example 1 (see page 150), which increased the dietary fibre content. Once the analysis is complete it is possible, if necessary, to make adjustments to the menu so it will comply with the nutritional guidelines. This may involve changing cooking methods, garnishes and adding more fibre foods or using alternative products.

Now do an analysis of a menu of your choice to determine whether it is low in fat, sugar and salt, and high in fibre. Use the lists given at the beginning of this appendix and the Healthy Eating Check table on p. 156.

Like the food groups menu check, this method is very simple and quick to execute, but can only give a guide not a detailed analysis. But it is hoped that it will also prove a useful check for the caterer/chef.

Healthy eating check using Appendix II, Example 2

Menu	Fat	Sugar	Salt	Dietary fibre
Whitebait	×			
White roll				
Butter	×			
Chicken sauté chasseur	×		×	
Glazed carrots	×		×	×
Dauphine potatoes	×		×	×
Glass of wine				
Chocolate gâteau and cream	×	×		
Coffee – cream and sugar	×	×		
Liqueur				
Added salt at table			× ×	
Total	8	2	5	2

Comments: Meal is high in fat content and low in sugar and dietary fibre. Heavy seasoning with salt will increase intake.

Healthy eating check

Menu	Fat	Sugar	Salt	Dietary fibre
Total				

Comments:

Useful books for further reading

Food tables

The Composition of Foods, Medical Research Council, HMSO 1978
Manual of Nutrition, ninth edition, Ministry of Agriculture, Fisheries and Food, HMSO 1985
Sainsbury's Food Facts, Sainsbury's stores or J. Sainsbury Ltd, Stamford House, Stamford Street, London SE1 9LL
Understanding Nutrition Information, Tesco stores or Tesco Stores Ltd, Delamore Road, Cheshunt, Herts EN8 9SL

Nutritional guidelines

Proposals for Nutritional Guidelines for Health Education in Britain, NACNE 1983, The Health Education Authority
Diet and Cardiovascular Disease, COMA Report on Health and Social Subjects 28, HMSO 1984
Nutritional Guidelines, ILEA, Heinemann Educational 1985
Dietary Reference Values for Food, Energy and Nutrients for the United Kingdom, COMA Report on Health and Social Subjects 41, HMSO 1991
Dietary Reference Values – A Guide, Department of Health, HMSO 1991

Theory of nutrition

Food and Nutrition, A. Tull, Oxford 1983
Human Nutrition, fourth edition, M.E. Barasi and R.F. Mottram, Hodder and Stoughton 1987
Theory of Catering, V. Ceserani and R. Kinton, Hodder and Stoughton 1986
Nutrition, Basic Concepts and Applications, W.L. Scheider, McGraw-Hill 1983
Diet and Nutrition, B.R. Ward, Life Guides, Franklin Watts 1987
Balancing your Diet, J. Salmon, Sainsbury's Food Guide 2, Sainsbury's 1982
Dictionary of Nutrition and Food Technology, A.E. Bender, Butterworths 1968

Food preservation

Food Science in Catering, G.V. Robins, Heinemann, 1982
Food Irradiation, T. Webb and T. Lang, Thorsons 1990
The New E for Additives, M. Hanssen and J. Marsden, Thorsons 1987
Danger Additives at Work, M. Miller, London Food Commission 1985

Healthy eating

Eating for Health, Health Depts, Great Britain and Northern Ireland, HMSO 1978
Eating for Health, C. Robbins, Granada 1985
The Healthy Catering Manual, C. Robbins, Dorling Kindersley 1989
Catering for Health, D.R. Stevenson and P.M. Scobie, Hutchinson 1987
Taste of Health, edited by J. Rogers, BBC 1985

Ethnic diets

Modern Jewish Cookery, A. der Haroutunian, Granada 1985
Samosa, P. Fisher, Forbes 1983
The Vegetarian Handbook, R. Doyle, Thorsons 1985
Vegetarian Catering, R. Davies, Gale Odgers 1987
Sarah Brown's Vegetarian Cookbook, S. Brown, Grafton 1986

Special diets

Human Nutrition and Dietetics, S. Davidson and R. Passmore, Churchill Livingstone 1979
Clinical Nutrition and Dietetics for Nurses, A.W. Goode, J.P. Howard and S. Woods, Unibooks 1985
The Gluten-Free Diet Book, P. Rawcliffe and R. Rolph, Martin Dunitz 1985
The Healthy Heart Diet Book, R. Longstaff and J. Mann, Optima 1988
The Salt Free Diet Book, G. MacGregor, Martin Dunitz 1984
Cooking for Diabetes, J. Metcalfe, Thorsons 1985
The Diabetic Cookbook, R. Longstaff and J. Mann, Martin Dunitz 1984

Useful addresses

Department of Health (Catering and Dietetic Advisors), Hannibal House, Elephant and Castle, London SE1 6TE

Health Education Authority, Hamilton House, Mabledon Place, London WC1A 9BD

HMSO, PO Box 276, London SW8 5DT

Hotel Catering & Institutional Management Association, 191 Trinity Road, London SW17 7HN

Scottish Health Education Group, Woodburn House, Canaan Lane, Edinburgh EG10 4SG

The British Diabetic Association, 10 Queen Anne Street, London W1M 0BD

The British Dietetic Association, 7th Floor, Elizabeth House, 22 Suffolk Street, Queensway, Birmingham B1 1LS

The British Nutrition Foundation, 15 Belgrave Square, London SW1

The Chief Rabbi, Alder House, Tavistock Square, London WC1H 9HP

The Coeliac Society of the United Kingdom, PO Box 181, London NW2 2QY (self-addressed envelopes only)

The Food Commission (UK) Ltd, 88 Old Street, London EC1V 9AR

The Islamic Foundation, 223 London Road, Leicester LE2 1ZE

The Sikh Cultural Society of Great Britain, 88 Mollison Way, Edgware, Middlesex HA8 5QN

The Vegetarian Society, Parkdale, Dunham Road, Altrincham, Cheshire WA14 4QG

Vegan Society, 33–35 George Street, Oxford OX1 2AY

Index